COMMON PRINT

Δ

Published by Common Print, September 2015.
ISBN 978-0-9930965-3-2

Printed and Bound in Great Britain by
Thomson the Printers, 14 Carnoustie Place,
Glasgow G5 8PB.

A Book of Ideas
2016-21

This book is based on Common Weal policy papers which can be found at allofusfirst.org/library (and some yet to be published papers). We thank all of those who have given their time to work on Common Weal policy reports. Special thanks for comment and guidance on specific sections of this book to: Iain Cairns, Gemma Bone, Oliver Escobar, Neal Lawson, Isobel Lindsay, Gordon Morgan, Stephen Elstub, Katherine Trebeck, Iain Black, Deirdrie Shaw, Pete Ritchie, Lesley Orr, Willie Sullivan, Andrew Cumbers, Geoff Whitham, Robert McMaster, Laurie McFarlane, David Comerford, Alexander Schwenk, Liz Murray, David Carr, Callum MacDonald, Duncan McCann, Peter McColl, Katie Gallogly-Swan, John Davis, Emma Ritch, Mike Danson, Gordon Maloney, Joe Brady, Scottish Human Rights Commission, Malcolm Fraser, and Policy Lab attendees on education and early years.

HELLO

...and welcome to Common Weal's Book of Ideas. The focus of this book is simple. There's a Scottish election in May 2016 which will elect a five-year government; so what could that government do over those five years using the powers the Scottish Parliament has (or is likely to have) to create an 'all of us first' society?

Part One of the book asks what we need to achieve to create that better Scotland. Part Two asks what we can do to make sure we achieve it. It is not a manifesto—that's for political parties to produce. And it's not a programme for government—though it would make a government that adopted a good proportion of these ideas an exciting and radical government. It is instead a 'pool' of ideas from which political parties can fish when they produce their own manifestos. No-one is expected to agree with all of it and none of it is put forward as the only way we can achieve change. So you may find yourself agreeing with an aim or a goal but think there is a better way to achieve it. That's great—let us hear about it.

Fundamentally, this book attempts to end the excuse that we can't do things differently in Scotland; that we don't have the power to change things, that 'aye been' is somehow good enough, and that competent management is the extent of our hopes and aspirations. Common Weal will follow this book with a series of policy papers explaining in more detail how some of the key proposals can be achieved. Until then, we hope it will leave you inspired to believe that a different, better Scotland is within our reach.

Contents

KEY
IDEAS

Tax, investment, and the public realm

#1   Raise the top tax band (from £150,000) from 45p to 50p, raising approximately £20m.

#2   Introduce new 43p tax band at income over £50,000, raising approximately £180m

#3   Abolish the Council Tax

#4   Give local authorities the power to set the rates of a local income tax, a property tax and a land value tax

#5   Over five years, cut the block grant to local government until it represents 50 per cent of current spending—and cut national income tax by exactly the same amount. Local government will then increase the rates of its local taxes to make up the difference, decentralising tax while keeping aggregate tax rates constant. A 50 per cent block grant will remain to enable equalisation and redistribution between local authorities.

#6   Land Value Tax would, however, have a minimum rate but a high threshold (per unit value) which would target wealth and unproductive use of land. This will raise approximately £500m. This will be cut from local government budgets and the £500m used to reduce the impact of budget cuts.

#7   Establish a Scottish National Investment Bank. The Scottish Government should securitise it to a total of £2bn and capitalise it using its annual borrowing powers of approximately £200m. A liquidity ratio of 10:1 would then mean the SNIB would be able to invest £20bn to the public and private sectors via a new mutual borrowing model.

#8 Create Special Purpose Vehicles (such as National Mutual Companies) to invest in big national interventions and to work around the severe borrowing limits on Holyrood.

#9 Create a charter of what is and isn't a core public service and maintain all core public services in full public control

#10 Commit to nationalising care over 15 years and begin by creating a National Childcare Service

#11 Focus childcare on a high-quality curriculum of play and emotional development

#12 Create a National Policy Academy for Organisation and Service Design to innovate the delivery of public services and improve public sector bureaucracy and organisation

#12 Create a parallel Scottish digital currency to inject £1 billion into the Scottish economy, putting £250 of additional, debt-free money into the hands of every Scottish citizen

#13 Establish a system of National Policy Academies which would be centres of excellence of new thinking in key areas of public policy, both to improve national debate and to act as a substantial resource to the civil service and others

#14 Create a specialist government 'legal hit squad' which would specialise in overcoming legal objections to public policy changes

#15 Publish a regular dashboard of indicators and always present key indicators such as GDP in this contextualised way

Democracy

#16   Transform existing 'local' authorities into regional councils (possibly with some mergers) and introduce a new layer of properly local councils with unpaid community politicians meeting in the evenings. Both of these layers of government would be serviced by the existing officer staff in the local authorities so there would be no need for expensive reorganisation

#17   To enable maximum devolution of powers as and when different councils wish to exercise those powers, a 'tree of reserved powers' would be produced for each level of government (Holyrood, regional councils, local councils) and any layer of government would be able to 'draw down' any powers which are not on that list—if they want to. This would take place within the framework of powerful national standards for service to ensure consistent and fair delivery of core services across the country

#18   Democratise these new regional authorities by requiring a full committee system open to the public, banning the use of ALEOs for delivering core services, supporting local journalism, and introducing citizen oversight committees

#19   Create a National Policy Academy dedicated to democratic innovation and staffed to be able to support and facilitate participatory democratic practices. These would be built around existing expertise (academics, secondments from the civil service and so on) and would be democratic and open, enabling anyone to become involved in discussing and shaping policy ideas

#20   Use the best practice in consultation via the Democracy Academy and let Academies lead in organising public deliberation

#21   Use mini-publics as the default way to provide advice to government, avoiding 'expert only panels'

#22   Use participatory budgeting where budgets are being set

#23   Create a network of 'tings': forums to discuss or create ideas driven and owned by citizens, and linked closely to the network of National Policy Academies

#24   Develop a national policy conference/ting to provide a national focus on the issues emerging from local tings

#25   End the use of commercial consultancy in advising government, instead using National Policy Academies

#26   Democratise the governance of public institutions by giving the identified communities they affect the right to vote for members of respective governing bodies

#27   Legislate to place on anyone engaged in lobbying in any layer of government in Scotland a duty to register the full budget of that lobbying campaign

#28   Explore a 'right of recall' power to enable citizens to challenge elected politicians under specified circumstances

#29   Create a digital media fund to support and encourage innovation in digital journalism including citizen journalism and alternative and independent news sites

#30   Develop a robust school curriculum on citizenship and participation throughout schooling

#31   Use local and national Tings for politicians, civil servants, the educational establishment, the institutionalised profession, local authorities, pupils, and parents to collaborate on the development of schooling in Scotland

#32   Explore the possibility of producing a kitemark to indicate businesses which have good industrial democracy practices

Economy

#33   Set out a national intention to rebalance the economy via an industrial policy, at the heart of which should be a commitment to direct intervention to stimulate Scottish industries which the market alone has failed to adequately develop

#34   Create a National Housing Company which would borrow against rents to build a new generation of public rental houses in Scotland limited in scale only by demand. It should also renovate existing properties by borrowing against future savings in energy costs from better insulation

#35   Create a National Energy Company which would borrow against future income from energy generation to build all new energy generation in Scotland in collective ownership. It should also create a manufacturing arm which would build as much as possible of the technology in Scotland

#36   Create a National Childcare Company and professionalise child development with the aim of creating more well-paid employment for women

#37   Create a national strategy for supporting micro-, small- and medium-scale manufacturing in Scotland. This should involve three elements. First a National Distribution and Export Company to enable these businesses to get effective market access. Second, create open-access manufacturing infrastructure. Third, develop a shared services facility to help smaller businesses manage IP and other legal matters.

#38   Promote an open source software business in Scotland, initially by moving public agencies to open source practices

#39   Create a national economic development approach which emphasises 'smart specialisation' and design-driven innovation. Create effective national design education to support this over the long term

#40   Linked to the deconsumerisation strategy, seek to develop the tourism industry by stimulating greater domestic tourism

#41   Introduce a Land Value Tax to bring land back to its economic value and in so doing increase the viability of land-based industries

#42   Move to a system of 'sector associations' to develop economic development approaches at an individual sector level. These would involve all players in the sector including staff, unions, customers, local communities and education providers as well as big and small businesses and supply chain businesses.

#43   Develop an 'industrial policy toolkit' with a range of possible actions which will help sector associations understand what powers and actions they can influence in developing plans.

National infrastructure, resilience and self-reliance

#44   Create municipal energy retail companies to democratise the retail energy market and reduce costs to suppliers (and in combination with a National Energy Company, to ensure Scotland's energy needs are met)

#45   Task the National Energy Company with producing a national heating strategy based on much greater reliance on renewables (such as biomass and solar thermal), less on imported gas, and to improve the efficiency of heating through solutions such as district heating

#46   Task the National Housing Company to develop a 'mortgage to rent' system to protect home owners in the event of unaffordable rises in mortgage costs when interest rates rise. The same model can be used to help those who wish to move from owning to renting but with continued tenancy of existing houses

#47   Make the control of house prices an explicit aim of the increased housing supply by the National Housing Company and set out the goal of controlling house price rises as a national priority

#48   Put in place a system of rent control in the private rental market to ensure reliable supply, and increase security of tenure through ending 'no fault' grounds for repossession and scrapping short-term tenancy contracts

#49   Develop a municipal banking sector offering households and small businesses supportive, local banking which does not seek to maximise profit through practices such as heavy marketing of loans

#50   Explore whether a national mutual approach to broadband and telecoms can be introduced in the future

#51   Put in place a package of measures to ensure 'food sovereignty'. This will include vertical integrated procurement approaches, effective distribution systems and possibly a food 'direct debit' scheme

#52   Create a National Policy Academy for Farming, Food and
        Agriculture to improve faming techniques and technologies in
        Scotland along 'agroecology' lines

#53   Institute a 'nextgen' transport strategy to prepare Scotland now
        for rapidly developing transport technologies

#54   Consider a Scottish leadership study to identify barriers
        which prevent people educated in Scotland from taking major
        leadership roles in the country

#55   Take remedial measures to protect refugees and asylum seekers
        within the confines of the UK asylum system, including decent
        housing and refusing Police Scotland's consent with dawn raids.

#56   Embed environmental performance factors into every element
        of policy development

#57   Create a National Academy for Conflict Resolution, Non-
        Violence, Peace, and international Relations

Economic and Social Equality and Poverty

#58   Give socioeconomic duty to sector associations and economic
        development agencies to promote economic equality in
        economic development

#59   Look at where government 'conditionality' can be used to
        encourage employers to take actions which reduce inequality
        and explore a 'kite mark' system or similar.

#60   Stimulate higher pay employment in traditionally feminine
        sectors of the economy, in particular childcare

#61 Provide better careers advice for girls and young women to encourage them to consider careers in traditionally male-dominated sectors, thereby desegregating the labour market over the longer term

#62 Design a Personal and Social Education (PSE) syllabus to move away from grades-focussed careers advice and towards a more holistic understanding of citizenship, human rights, inequality, and self-reflexivity.

#63 Put in place free national childcare support to make careers for parents (and in particular women) easier

#64 Promote a model of 'better businesses for women', for example with family-friendly hours and reporting on pay equality

#65 Place a gender equality duty on economic development agencies

#66 Make employment tribunals on sex discrimination free

#67 Take a human rights-focussed approach to all equalities issues and embed human rights in all public practices

#68 Always set a good example on equalities in public life through all actions of public agencies

#69 Make empathy education, conflict resolution and violence reduction key aspects of the Scottish school curriculum

#70 Ensure proper funding for women's refuge shelters to support women and children who have suffered from domestic abuse.

#71 Do not use welfare top-ups as a means of dealing with the failures of the UK benefits system but instead invest substantially in hardship funds

#72   Consider a scheme which would provide cash payments for the young unemployed who participate in a community improvement volunteer scheme

#73   Task the National Housing Company with ensuring sufficient supply of very affordable rental housing to mitigate the effects of poverty

#74   Mitigate the problems of fuel poverty by reducing energy costs via a system of municipal energy companies

#75   Create a legal 'right to food' to create a legal framework for tackling food poverty

#76   Consider large scale collective bulk purchasing options (linked to the National Distribution Company) to reduce the cost of core staple foods to mitigate poverty

#77   Explore a 'public cafe' scheme to provide inexpensive good food in a cafe setting focussed on areas with high rates of food poverty

#78   Pursue a consistent strategy of 'Asset Based Community Development' in which regeneration is put in the hands of local communities through ownership and management of physical and human assets

#79   Create a policy of locating the manufacturing industries stimulated by the industrial policy close to communities that are in particular need of good jobs

#80   Ensure all public housing has high-quality disability access through the National Housing Company and change the work programme to support the most isolated into work.

#81 Set-up a National Policy Academy for Equality

Quality of life

#82   Change policy in the planning process to reorientate it towards
       public good and away from private profit

#83   Increase the quality of all housebuilding both through the
       manufacture of public rental housing in German-style house
       factories via the National Housing Company and by increasing
       building standards

#84   Create a National Housing and Transport Policy Academy. This
       Academy should then advise on new ways to develop and build
       towns, cities and communities focussed on good design and
       quality of life—not short-term private profit

#85   As well as setting a specific goal of controlling house prices
       through supply, set a specific goal of desegregating housing
       along socioeconomic lines though mixed community planning

#86   Make sure that all management of public rental housing is
       extremely local, to the block or street level. Where possible
       build in a concierge system

#87   Set out the aim of improving the aesthetic quality and general
       environment of housing and communities, with a 'zero
       tolerance of grim' mentality. Consider creating a community
       improvement volunteer service to carry out works such as
       painting, landscaping and developing facilities

#88   Take a 'nextgen' approach to the development of the town
       centre and how services and facilities are provided

#89   Make a key part of a transport nextgen approach to connect communities with services, facilities, the arts and other social goods

#90   Set out a national deconsumerisation strategy. This would involve promoting activities such as learning, crafts, hobbies, domestic travel, sport, participation in the arts, and so on. It would focus on making participation possible (transport, childcare, local democracy, investment in facilities) and cheaper ('shareshops', tool libraries, cheaper public access to cultural and sporting facilities). More access to land to create more facilities such as parks, sports pitches, and allotments should also be targeted.

#91   There should be a national skills database and learning for fun strategy

#92   Put in place a national strategy for improving participation in the arts, both as audience and artist

#93   Do what is possible in public bodies to control marketing and advertising, particularly near children

#94   Explore a 'direct debit' scheme for food purchasing to sustain better quality food production and healthier eating

#95   Explore the possibility of devising a form of Citizen's Income for artists

#96   Seek audience expansion in arts through school, transport and by exploiting the low marginal cost of extra performances

#97   Stimulate a wide range of creative professions by revisiting proposals for a Scottish national digital channel

#98   Allow football fans to take over their clubs and bring them into fan ownership if a majority vote in favour of it.

#99   See criminal justice as a quality of life issue and pursue policy approaches which improve communities' quality of life rather than approaches which emphasise punishment. This will lead to an assumption against jail and an end to short sentences altogether

#100   See policing also as a quality of life issue. Other than the small proportion of police activity which is national in scale, make policing extremely localised with policy and practice set by police working with local councils, and move away from criminalisation policies like stop-and-search.

#101   Put quality of life at the heart of education. Place the emphasis on positive, happy development of pupils, not testing or other practices which create anxiety. Testing should only happen at the very end of school—if at all. Work should be project-based (not subject-based) and learning should be drawn out of project work.

Part One

HOW SHOULD WE CARRY OURSELVES?

Chapter One
Putting all of us first

The urge to imagine and to build a better society is part of human nature. The opportunity to build something better is always in our hands. But another part of human nature, cautious or selfish, tells us it's too hard, it's too risky, now isn't the time, the people don't want it, or we can't afford it. This battle between our instincts—to put all of us first or to put me first—defines us. For a lifetime power and money have spoken to our worst instincts. We are surrounded by adverts that encourage us to be greedy, newspapers which encourage us to mistrust those weaker than us, corporations which demand that we do as we're told and politicians who either like it that way or seem paralysed in the face of this me-first world.

It's not what people say they want. They say they want a secure, affordable home in a community where they can enjoy going outside to a clean and healthy environment. They say they want to be healthy and to feel good, to know they'll have enough money to pay the bills and to buy what they need and to know that they'll have that financial security in the future. They want meaningful, secure, satisfying work they care about. They want good relationships with family and friends and to know those they care about are safe and secure. They want to be part of a community and to know that the other members of that community are also cared for, safe and secure. They want access to green and wild spaces, community spaces and play areas; to arts, hobbies and leisure activities; to good transport links. They want good facilities and high-quality services locally when they need them. They want to have human rights, to be free from discrimination, to be accepted and respected. To live a good life.

We hear much about a politics of aspiration. Well, these are our aspirations: home, work, security, community, recreation, public service and respect. What has me-first politics given us? Profiteering, competition, elitism, greed, anger, blame and mistrust. All over the world me-first politics are failing and all over the world people are looking for something better. They want a society that puts all of us first.

Nowhere has a better chance to build that new society than Scotland does now. In 2016 Scotland will hold an election. It will elect a five-year government. That government will not have some of the powers it would need to really change society, and some of those missing powers (on social security, wages, regulation, control of money and the big economic powers) are crucial while others (like defence and international representation) rule out entire areas of decision-making. It will also be facing the impacts of major cuts in public funding and financial attacks on the least wealthy in society. But it will still be a powerful government with a substantial range of powers and a considerable (though overstretched) budget. There is plenty it can do.

What no-one should argue is that Scotland isn't ready. Since the politics of this nation fundamentally changed during the independence referendum, every sign suggests that the people who live and work in Scotland really do want a different way of running society. Perhaps those in other nations may say that now is not their time, that there isn't the support for change. No-one can say that in Scotland. A lazy, self-interested, sterile politics which spoke the language of me-first has been punished. A new politics which has spoken the language of all of us first has been rewarded. Now it must deliver.

Because a moment of change and a moment of history are not the same thing. Scotland faces a moment of change—but it will only become a moment of history if that opportunity to change is grasped. For three years, Scotland has talked excitedly and passionately about change. But change isn't a slogan, it's an action; you do it or you don't. The time to talk about change has come to an end and the time to make it happen is upon us. Change does not mean slightly different management of what is already there, or trying to prevent the wrong kind of change. Change means that the 'facts on the ground' change. If people are left to live the same way we lived before they will rightly be angry, rightly disappointed. Look at those aspirations, and make them real, or face the consequences.

So how can this be done? Throughout history, there have been two basic ideas about how to create a better future. One believes in progress through conflict. It isn't that conflict isn't healthy and creative—it certainly can be, particularly when the conflict moves both sides forward and can be resolved. Unfortunately, that is not the kind of conflict me-first politics pursues. The model of progress they favour is survival of the 'fittest'—and only of the 'fittest'.

The idea is that if you have two alternative options you should encourage them to try and defeat each other, with whichever one survives clearly being 'the best'. If you do that enough times then weakness will be defeated and strength will be rewarded, leaving behind only the best. The only role of government is to keep out of the way, since working together rather than against each other simply encourages weakness. In this view of the world, schools are there to sort the 'strongest' children from the 'weakest', police and prisons are there to keep the 'wrong' people away from the 'right' ones, the 'best' economy lets the biggest businesses bully the smallest, and low taxes are important so that 'successful' people are not dragged down by the need to support 'unsuccessful' people. Above all, there is a single measure of strength and it is profit. A person that achieves more wealth must be better than someone who achieves less wealth (even if that person is a nurse or a teacher who made a decision not to seek personal profit). A business that makes more profit must be better than a business that makes less profit (even if the profitable business has made its money underpaying staff, destroying the environment, damaging communities or putting competitors out of business through corrupt practices).

If this sounds like a charter for bullies and cheats, a self-fulfilling prophecy, that's because it is. In me-first theory, what is left behind are the businesses which are most productive—the ones who are most efficient at producing and distributing goods and services for our collective good. But in Britain this is the opposite of what has happened. Quite predictably, by favouring short-term gamesmanship over long-term investment we are left with an economy that pays as little as possible, invests as little as possible, and extracts as much wealth out of the economy as possible—all in the shortest possible time. Our economy does not use money to make things, it uses money to take money from others. We don't have better houses, we have more expensive houses. We don't have better transport, we have much more expensive transport. We don't have manufacturing (which creates wealth through skill and investment), we have corporate banking and corporate retail, whose business models largely rely on capturing more and more of existing markets so they can transfer the maximum amount of wealth from their customers to themselves.

The other idea about how to achieve progress is to do it through mutuality. Mutuality is the belief that people have more interests in common than they do which divide them, and that people tend to be more effective if they're working together than if they are working against each other. It does not mean that there is no competition in society—competition can be healthy and positive. It just does not turn competition into an obsession, converting what is healthy and positive into a destructive war of all against all. It does this by recognising that even competitors will have more interests that bring them together than separate them. For example, two businesses working in the field of computer programming may well find themselves competing for the same contracts. But before they do, to be healthy businesses they both need certain things—good transport links; a stable, supportive banking system; universities that turn out high-skill programmers; a public sector that makes it possible for their small businesses to compete for contracts and so on. A mutual approach recognises that of course eventually these two businesses will be in competition, but until then, everyone benefits if we all work together to create the best possible environment for both of these companies to succeed.

A mutual approach also recognises that massive concentrations of wealth and resources are inefficient and unproductive. Think about a nursery school. If you want the children to build, what would be the best strategy? Allow the biggest child to push, bully and snatch from the other children until he has all of the building blocks? Clearly not, because the game has become about snatching and hoarding, not building. If the building blocks are shared out more evenly across all of the children in the class, some will hoard it, but most will build something. On average, a more equal distribution of wealth and resources will lead to more productivity. If more ordinary Scots could get access to land, how many more land-based businesses would they create? If more start-up businesses could get secure, supportive loans, how many more would survive and grow? If more medium-sized businesses could beat big corporations to win contracts to supply the public sector with goods and services, how many more jobs could they create?

Societies which favour me-first ideas lose their public spaces, parks, and facilities. They create more and more low-pay jobs, and have more and more of the wealth created in their economies extracted and not reinvested. They create poorer-quality public services in favour of more and more pressure to spend on consumer goods that people don't need, and don't really want. They always end up with poverty and they always end up harming their environment—"what profit is there in looking after an environment?" they say.

Societies which favour all-of-us-first policies have much lower levels of inequality and poverty, much stronger public services and facilities, much better public spaces, and better environments. But these things you would expect. What is surprising is that almost everything becomes better in all-of-us-first societies—they have lower levels of crime, lower levels of mental health problems, higher levels of trust, higher levels of participation in civic life, better human rights... In fact there is almost no indicator which does not suggest that all-of-us-first societies are better for more or less all of their citizens.

How does this happen? It is a simple loop to understand. First, economies managed in a mutual manner have much more variety of type and size of enterprise in them. They are dominated much less by low-pay, low-productivity, low-investment corporations and much more by independent businesses of many sizes. These businesses extract much less wealth from the economy and invest much more of their profits back into the economy, are more productive (not least because they are much more likely to be involved in manufacturing), and are more innovative. This means that they create jobs which are much more skilled than those in me-first economies (the pursuit of fast profits does not favour investment in staff) and the economies as a whole produce much lower differences in wealth between the richest and poorest. These high-pay, more equal jobs make the average worker much wealthier and more-or-less prevent the problem of in-work poverty. Wealthier citizens then pay more tax. This is true even if taxes don't rise—if Scotland had the more equal wage structure of the best of the all-of-us-first economies, it would take in more than £4 billion of extra tax without raising tax rates at all, simply because people have more money in their pockets. But all of the evidence suggests that once you create a high-pay society, people choose to pay more in tax, because as they become more prosperous they realise that many of the things they really want come from public investment. So they are happy to make that investment. This means that they have very healthy public finances which are then invested into first-rate public services and first-rate public infrastructure. This infrastructure and these services then create strong, cohesive communities and high levels of public trust—in each other and in all the layers of government. And of course, high levels of public trust are great for the economy. So is lots of investment in public services and public infrastructure. This produces an economy with much more variety of business types and sizes—and so on...

There are many other consistent features of all-of-us-first societies which support this virtuous loop. They have strong industrial democracy with widespread trade union membership and collective bargaining. They have supportive but strong regulation of business to prevent them breaking this virtuous loop. They keep key infrastructure (like their energy networks) in public ownership.

There is absolutely no reason we can't achieve this in Scotland. We have a highly educated population and a very substantial capacity to innovate. We have good public services and pretty good national infrastructure (though our public services are under severe funding pressure and our local infrastructure has been steadily eroded). We have excellent natural resources and many elements of our economy provide a solid foundation for productive growth. But the most important thing is that the citizens of Scotland have responded enthusiastically to politicians who have spoken about an all-of-us-first future. The will is there.

So what should we do? This book will outline a series of ideas about how we can use the next five years of devolved government in Scotland to take big steps forward towards an all-of-us-first society— and to transform lives as we do it. All of these ideas can be done within the powers of the Scottish Parliament: everything comes with a simple explanation of how it can be done and how it can be paid for, and everything is based on successful models which have worked in other places. This does not mean these ideas are dogmatic—there is more than one way to achieve some of them (for example, locally-owned social enterprises or managed by local authorities, tax rates set locally or nationally etc.). But the outcomes are specific.

It is based around a major programme of investment, particularly public and collective investment, in areas which will quickly more than repay that investment. We must stimulate the economy and create high-pay jobs by making major investment in things like housebuilding, renewable energy technology manufacture, and childcare. We need the infrastructure to enable us to make that investment, such as a National Investment Bank, and a reliable local municipal banking sector plus national companies to raise finance. We need to strengthen universal collective provision of services—which means we need to be clever with tax and with innovation in public organisations. If we can make big public organisations flatter with more front-line control over strategy and policy, that 'circular power' will improve innovation and efficiency. Because Scotland has such an unequal and low-pay economy (three out of five people in work earn less than £25,000 a year) it is difficult to raise additional income using income tax alone. However, with a package of tax measures and the introduction of some new taxes (along with decentralising tax powers), money can be raised to prevent the worst of the cuts which are being imposed on Scottish public services.

Then we need to fix Scotland's shocking centralisation by putting in place powerful community politics and by giving citizens much more direct say in how democracy works. We need to localise our economies again and ensure that more of the decisions about Scotland's future lie in Scotland's hands by exerting much more direct control over areas of essential national wellbeing such as transport, food, energy, banking, and housing. We need to encourage innovation everywhere, not least in public policy and in public services. We need an economic policy that emphasises domestically-owned, productive, high-skill enterprises which focus on 'smart specialisation'—working out what niche you're particularly good at and doing it really well. But we also need to give enterprises in every part of the economy (however mundane or routine they appear) a chance to work mutually to improve their businesses and shape the business environment in which they work.

We need to do everything we can to tackle the unacceptable poverty that is being created across Scotland by bad economic and social policies. This will be hard—Scotland does not have any of the major powers in this area. But we can put in place systems which support those affected with money and support services. We can also mitigate some of the impacts through provision of better and cheaper housing, with much more fuel efficiency, and with collective fuel and food purchasing arrangements to reduce the cost of living. We can take a radical new approach to community development by giving people control of assets and budgets so they can become active in regenerating their own communities (and can also keep more of the investment made in their communities). We can give every part of government a specific socio-economic duty to use all of the powers at their disposal to reduce poverty, and we can create the resource of a powerful National Policy Academy for Equality and Poverty.

We should set out a package of policies on equality. We need first-rate childcare so more women can be fully active in the economy and in society if they want to be. We need to close the gap in male and female pay first by intervening to create better paid jobs in sectors of the economy where many women work (paying for professional-level childcare in the new childcare sector would be an important start). Segregating the economy between 'male' jobs and 'female' jobs is the main problem in the pay differential between the sexes—so we must desegregate the labour market with a major programme of careers advice to encourage women into high-pay parts of the economy such as design, technology, engineering and manufacturing. We should also be doing whatever we can to encourage good industrial democracy. This will be hard because all of the powers are reserved. But it is through strong industrial democracy that workers are better able to negotiate a fair pay and to help innovate their workplace—both crucial in reducing wage inequality. And we must tackle negative social attitudes to difference (including race, religion, sexuality, gender, disability and nationality) by putting much more emphasis on empathy education, teaching conflict resolution and by pursuing violence reduction strategies.

Then we must put all of our focus on constantly questioning whether our public and collective policy decisions are making the quality of life better or worse for citizens. Housing and town planning must become first and foremost about making the places we live better, happier, more social, and more beautiful. We need people to have quick and easy access to great local facilities and amenities, support learning and participation in the arts, and deconsumerise (policies which encourage people to be more active and participative and to spend less of their time and money just shopping). We should improve work-life balance, make food something which enhances our lives and the environment, build up domestic tourism, and encourage people to be involved in shaping their own communities. We need a policing and justice system which is not focussed on punishment but on quality of life for communities—which means working with them and being deeply embedded in them—and an end to failing, punitive prison sentences where there are better alternatives. And we need to re-orientate education as fundamentally about supporting young people to become the best and happiest citizens they can be, where attainment (what a child has achieved) is more important than assessment (measuring how well a child can answer).

This package of actions should kick-start the positive loop discussed above. Thousands of properly paid jobs can be created in childcare, housebuilding, energy technology manufacture and instillation through direct investment. Policies that localise economies will transfer wealth from corporations to small businesses. Economic development approaches which boost manufacture and encourage people to buy more domestically (and locally) produced goods will create many more good jobs. These will increase tax revenues and reduce the burden on social services, reduce poverty (with direct intervention to address the most acute impacts of the attacks on the income of the poorest), and reduce income and gender inequality. These policies will hand real power back to communities, put the emphasis on people's feelings of security (economic and social), and focus on what makes life more enjoyable and rewarding.

We will get to a Common Weal future through creativity, enterprise, equality, security, responsibility, decency, and joy.

Some of the proposals in this book can be seen in embryonic form in Scotland already. Some bits may have been tried out in studies or exist in watered-down form. These are all strong bases from which to build. This book does not assess how far along the way to achieving some of these outcomes we are. Nor does it offer detailed implementation plans (to be published following up on the book). It is a book of ideas, not a manifesto—those are for political parties to produce. It is a series of visions of what facts on the ground we must change and how we should change them. That does not mean it is vague. It is unlikely that 'sort of' will work. It's not just doing something, it's doing it in the right way. It's how it should have been done in the first place. And yes, it will mean that a few noses will be put out of joint. But then, that's the nature of change.

Scotland has just been through three transformative years. The country is still divided on its constitutional future. But acting now to turn the transformation in our national debate into a transformation of our society is something that can unite both sides. For those who did not support independence in 2014, it will improve their society in ways that they say they want it to be improved. It will show that the aspirations to be a better society were not just rhetoric and that this is a sincere project which is about making their lives better, right now.

For those who did support independence, it is a chance to push the boundaries of what Scotland can do; to show that yes, there is more we can do to change Scotland but there is also a lot we can't do. The Scotland achieved through this programme of ideas would be much more robust, much more self-reliant and be in a much stronger position to make a case for why it needs the remainder of those powers in the future.

The urge to imagine and build a better society is shared by more than one side in Scotland's current political debate. But it will take one side to step forward and make it happen. Because nothing 'just happens': things don't just 'fix themselves', infrastructure and institutions don't get built spontaneously, innovations don't just occur. People roll up their sleeves and work hard at creating them, facing down those from across the political spectrum who say that nothing can be done. Then they happen. And perhaps above all, Scotland will not become better just because wealth has been created. After all, RBS created plenty wealth— and little good that did us. It's not about someone being rich, it's about all of us being prosperous. It's not about profit for a few, but about investment for us all. To quote the song, it's not about what you've been given, it's what you do with what you've got. Scotland is already a rich nation. So what are we going to do with it?

Let's choose to use that wealth to improve all of our lives and that those lives should be happy and healthy. Let's use wealth in common for the wellbeing of all. Which in old Scots has a name.

Common Weal.

Chapter Two
The tasks and the tools

Before we begin to look at the individual ideas which this book suggests shape the best possible future for Scotland, it is always worth thinking about the tasks at hand. This helps to guide us in the choices we need to make as we put ideas into practice. Here are 12 tasks which lie ahead.

One: create a design-driven future. Me-first politics is obsessed with the idea that the main role that society collectively should take is to leave well alone and let the powerful do as they please (though they translate it into French and call it laissez-faire to make it sound like a better idea than it is). They think that as long as those 'winners' from the battle of all against all that they encourage are left alone to do whatever they want, the outcome will be the best possible outcome. If that was to be true though, those 'winners' would mainly need to be interested in creating a future which is good for all of us—which is seldom how they 'won' in the first place. But even then, a whole lot of different people doing whatever they want is very rarely a good way to get anything done. The best future isn't going to be made out of uncoordinated actions by wealthy individuals, it is going to be designed. Design means working out what you want to achieve and producing a comprehensive, thought-through plan for how to do it. That means that if you want a better health service, design one, don't just put in place more performance indicators and hope it will arrive by luck. It means that if you want a more effective economy, the products and services it produces must be designed to be better than those produced by others, not just the same stuff sold with fancier advertising. It means that if you want your towns and cities to be beautiful we must plan them together, not just let corporations stick up skyscrapers wherever they want and dump dull, repetitive housing schemes wherever they can make profit. We must collectively decide what kind of public spaces and skylines we want to live among—and then we must design them. Designing better is an all-of-us-first impulse where a me-first impulse is simply to reduce the cost of what you already have. Scotland has an enviable history of design and innovation. It will be at the heart of an enviable future—if only we can put design back at the very heart of Scotland's collective life.

Two: improve economic equality. The reasons why economic equality is so important were discussed in chapter 1, but the answer is fairly straightforward—because it makes almost everything better for almost everyone. Improving economic equality happens as a result of many things, but primary among them is a tax and investment system with regulation that encourages a high-pay economy, and industrial democracy which enables employees to share in the wealth created. Only one of these will be in Scotland's hands (tax and investment), and that only in a limited way. So we need to be clever and focussed on making economic equality a target for all parts of government if we want to realise change. In one area, we can continue to ensure that people experience the effects of equality, and that is in providing universally available public services. When services are targeted at only the poor, they are almost always poor-quality services because society as a whole does not have as great a vested interest. When services are targeted at everyone, everyone has a vested interest in making them the best services possible. And when services are really good, they not only lift everyone up, they lift up the poorest much more than everyone else, helping to level the playing field. Universalism is perhaps the single biggest factor since the second world war in reducing the gaps between how the wealthy and the poor experience life. We must fight to protect it at all costs.

Three: achieve social equality. We continue to have a society in which some groups do not experience real equality. It is particularly true of the disabled, people from different racial and religious backgrounds, people with different sexualities or gender identities and women (who of course make up by far the biggest group which experiences inequality). One of the most effective ways to achieve greater social equality is to achieve greater economic equality. But there are other things we must do to. We must ensure appropriate laws enshrine the rights of groups that face inequality—and those rights must be policed and protected. We also have to face up to discriminatory attitudes and behaviours. We should make empathy education, conflict resolution training and anti-violence approaches at the heart of our education system. But we must also identify and fix the places where groups such as women are underrepresented in terms of access to power and decision-making. The next generation must grow up not only rejecting prejudice and powerlessness, but teaching the generations that came before them how these structures operate, and that they are not okay.

Four: ensure social security. The concept is easy to grasp—a good society should make everyone feel safe and secure in their lives. This means that no-one should be afraid of not having the essentials of life: shelter, warmth, food, respect. But even more importantly, no-one should have to fear not having these things in the future if their circumstances change. Losing a job or becoming ill or unable to work is not a reason for someone to fear hunger and cold. In fact, the constant fear of how to pay the bills and protect your loved ones is a form of psychological abuse that should not be accepted. Nor should we accept the fear of violence or the fear of being a victim of crime. The aim of policing and the justice system should be to achieve security for everyone. Some of us will be unlucky and face bad illnesses in our lives and these may give us good cause to fear the future. No-one else should.

Five: exert common control. We are an educated, democratic society. We have the ability and right to exert our collective power over the world around us with the aim of making that world better for all of us. We should use it. It is not enough to simply say "oh well, this bad thing happened and that's life"—it is our duty to work out why the bad thing happened, and to use all the tools at our collective disposal to make sure it doesn't happen again. And we have plenty of tools. We can encourage more national and local self-sufficiency so we are not permanently victims of the whims of globalised markets. We can regulate to ensure that, for example, corruption in the banking sector is not allowed to drag us all down. And where the market is making a mess of things we have the capacity to nationalise or mutualise, to take collective ownership and then to clean up the mess.

Six: control the commons. This collective capacity to design a future, exert control and shape our society is the commons. But while it can influence and direct things on our behalf, it is only truly ours if we control it. That is where democracy is so important. A state should never be anything more than an agreement between its citizens, and its citizens

14

should always have the ability to command the state—not the other way round. A modern system of national, local and participatory democracy means that we really can control the commons for ourselves.

Seven: build a common economy. The economy is a part of society. An economy is a system of 'social provisioning'—which just means that it is a means of producing and distributing the socially useful goods and services that a society needs. Society is the boss, not the economy. If an economy is not making its society better for all, it is failing. So our economy is failing. What a common economy should look like will be explored further in chapter five, but it is based on eradicating poverty through productivity, innovation, collective intervention, and by creating more ethical and localised markets, all of which produce better paid jobs. A common economy is an essential part of the foundation of a good society.

Eight: build common infrastructure. You can have common infrastructure or you can have private infrastructure. Private infrastructure has the sole purpose of making profit, which means finding ingenious ways to take your money from you (£1 to drop someone off at the airport?). Common infrastructure is about creating a high-functioning modern society. In recent years me-first politicians have made much of the idea that who owns and operates our infrastructure doesn't matter, so long as it's there. This is nonsense. That infrastructure (transport links and roads, postal services and communication technology, local amenities, schools and hospitals, public services and all the rest) should be designed to create a modern, effective, seamless environment with the sole purpose of improving our lives and helping us to be more creative and productive. Instead we have fragmented, privatised and under-resourced infrastructure, which is certainly improving things for the corporations that own them—just not us. Our infrastructure is a common good: we must design it, invest in it, and control it in common too.

Nine: prioritise strength and stability. From the level of very local community to entire nation state, the me-first view is that the only source of security and stability is to ensure the unhindered control of the supply of goods and services by global corporations. Any form of localism (being able to be more self-sufficient by producing more of your essential goods and services in your own local economy) is shunned. This is dangerous. As we have seen recently, big corporations which have almost entirely monopolised some of life's essentials (food, energy, housing, banking, clothing, transport) are not as bulletproof as they pretend they are. One supermarket chain can pull out of a town leaving no local supply of food. Banks can just close. Bulk house-builders just don't build houses when there is no profit, even if the social need is high. Fragmented, privatised energy markets are producing increased fears of blackouts. And all of this globalisation is enormously environmentally and socially harmful, as goods we used to produce ourselves are shipped to us from the other side of the world from producers which show little interest in human rights. The localism agenda is not luddite; creating resilient economies in strong, stable communities and localising production to protect the environment and the rights of producers is sensible.

Ten: promote good health. We have come to see health as a remedial issue, as if our common role is only to fix people if they get ill. But the causes of ill health are in everything we do. Globalised food markets feed us heavily processed food laden with fat, sugar, and salt. Hyper-consumerism has encouraged a sedentary lifestyle lacking exercise. The constant psychological pressure of consumerism through advertising and of unhealthy relationships to work damage our mental health. Our disempowering society in which we have declining control over our lives creates alienation and further mental health problems for all of us. And of course poverty brings a whole series of even more acute health problems. We need to see promoting our common good health as a thread running through everything we do, and we must stop turning a blind eye when decisions we make are clearly harming public health.

Eleven: design for life. Put simply, the me-first generation has scoured every aspect of our lives to seek to identify how more profit can be derived. The process of commercialising almost all aspects of our lives has been relentless. We can't take our children to play parks (which are often no longer there) so we pay to take them to soft play. We can't get books out of libraries which don't exist so we have to buy them. Airports are places used to strip as much money from us as possible. In a sharp return to the Victorian age, trains are designed to segregate us into those who can pay most and those who can pay least. Houses are not places in which to live but assets which we must redesign our lives around. A high quality of life is simply not achieved this way. We must take common control over our society and redesign it not for someone else's profit but for the quality of our own lives.

Twelve: recognise common decency. Margaret Thatcher remains the empress of me-first. One of the most honest things she ever said was that "economics are the method: the object is to change the soul". The me-first project tried to change society, but every bit as much, it tried to change us. It needs us not just to tolerate the vicious war of all against all, it needs us to support it, to believe in it, to want it. So the common aspects of our lives were broken down and were replaced with private alternatives. They encouraged us to be greedy, to mistrust each other, to change our values, and not to care about others. They weakened the social institutions that brought us together. They created media rules which enabled them and their supporters to dominate the ownership of the media. They left us little choice but to go along with it. It is for the all-of-us-first generation to win back the human soul from the me-firsters. We must rebuild the institutions which bind us and tackle the structures which divide us. But perhaps above all we must not be afraid to fight for the quality of our collective souls. There is nothing wrong with wanting to look after your family; there is something wrong about not caring about other people's families. There is nothing wrong in having aspiration for yourself; there is something wrong about not caring about people who are suffering. We must fight for common decency and we must not shrink from saying openly that it is a major part of the battle for an all-of-us-first society.

So if these are twelve tasks we must set ourselves in creating an all-of-us-first society, what are the tools with which we can do it? The following are ten sets of tools that we can use, all of which will be explored further at different points in this book.

One: democracy tools. We can use a wide range of well-developed tools to enable citizens to shape the common decisions which are made on their behalf by all layers of government and their agencies. We need a new layer of community democracy, and should make much better use of mini-public tools (where sample-sized cross sections of the public as a whole are allowed to make decisions and offer advice). We should have national processes of common decision-making, and we should use technology to enable this. The 'highborn state' in which one class of people are entitled to make decisions on behalf of all of us for our own good and in perpetuity (very few parts of the state are elected and many parts barely have democratic oversight) has no remaining justification. The generals and sirs and spooks and lords may once have claimed that there were no alternatives to their perpetual rule. We now have all the tools we need to change that.

Two: decision-making tools. Democracy tools are decision-making tools, but there still need to be day-to-day decisions made throughout our public institutions. The structures through which these decisions are made continue to be very top-down and are obsessively regimented by management speak of performance indicators and market discipline. However, as we shall see in chapter five, most of the best decision-making and even more of the best innovation does not come from managers but front-line staff. This has been shown conclusively in the private sector and it is no less true in the public sector. Tools which promote 'circular power', in which power to make decisions flows upwards from the front line as well as downwards from the management class are well developed. We must use these to flatten decision-making processes, enrich them with much more detailed and real knowledge than performance indicators, and promote innovation driven by the people who best see what must be innovated.

Three: thinking tools. As part of making decisions we must think deeply about what we are trying to achieve and how best we can do it. Vision and thinking about the future have been pushed out of public life in me-first politics, which teaches that this task is for the rich to carry out via their corporations—remember, the market will 'automatically' produce perfection so there's no point thinking about it. This book will propose a range of tools, from public Academies where we can collectively think about answers to the big questions to 'tings' (local parliaments where anyone can come together and think about solutions) to 'labs' (a short and focussed practical tool where people have a set period of time to produce creative solutions to specific problems). And in all of this we must not be afraid of 'next-gen' solutions. Sometimes we must accept that we are so far behind the best practice available that by the time we catch up, everything will have moved on again. The best response is to 'skip a generation' and start now to plan and redesign alternatives.

Four: investment tools. Chapter three will make the argument that where speculation is at the heart of me-first politics, investment is at the heart of all-of-us-first politics. But Scotland's parliament has very limited investment powers. The most powerful investment tools are taxation and public borrowing. Without proper control over these, additional investment tools are required. A priority must be a National Investment Bank for Scotland. Investing in local economies will be greatly improved if we have a municipal banking sector. But some of the big investments we need to make (especially in housing and energy) will require Scotland to be creative. 'Special purpose vehicles' are company structures which enable specific tasks to be pursued without risk to others. If we wish to do things on behalf of all citizens but government isn't allowed to do it, we can create National Mutual Companies to act like SPVs. These would be private companies but wholly democratically controlled by citizens. Ideally, they would be companies in which every citizen holds a single non-transferable share, is able to vote on all major decisions made by the company, and receives a dividend from that company. These might require agreement from the UK government and that might well be withheld. In that case a trustee ownership structure would be put in place where the constitution of the company gives all Scottish citizens voting rights at the AGM. These National Mutuals would have unlimited borrowing powers and be exempt from the me-first trade and procurement rules which have steadily privatised much of the public sector.

Investment also means gaining access to resources. A key resource is land and we should use our collective right to grant the permission to develop land (through planning permission, which is a collective right). This will open up access to land resources for the common good, such as by zoning land for social housing only, or by specifying the kind of economic activity it can be developed for. Where crucial assets are needed for collective investment but access to that resource is being blocked (for example so-called 'land banking' where corporations buy land for the explicit purpose of preventing their competitors from getting access to it), we should put in place a 'use it or lose it' law. If resources are not developed within a set period of time, we should immediately have the right to compulsorily purchase those resources for collective use. A strong community right to buy should be part of this.

Five: capacity tools. Me-first politics does not believe that it is important for a society to be able to manage itself; it would much rather that society was managed by global corporations. But having the domestic capacity to run your own affairs is sensible and being able to ensure the social security of your citizens is an important part of the role of common action. But that means we must have the capacity to manage being more self-sufficient. There are tools which can help with this, such as variations on the build-operate-train model. This means that if you wish to develop the ability to carry out an activity domestically but do not currently have the capacity (for example to create and operate modern 'house factories'), you can contract a private sector company to set up and run that infrastructure on our collective behalf. But unlike the usual privatisation model, a training programme with a predefined exit point would mean that at the end of the contract the domestic capacity to maintain that infrastructure is there. There are other similar 'mentor' models which can be used, including closer working with governments elsewhere which have necessary expertise (for example, a partnership with Denmark might be considered to help develop universal free childcare owned and run collectively). These are known as public-public partnerships.

In addition, during the referendum there was controversy around whether too many key posts in Scottish public life were filled by people from outside of Scotland. It is perfectly reasonable to explore how to ensure that Scotland creates a pool of domestic talent which is not only capable of doing these jobs well, but is capable of competing with the best in the world in securing those jobs. Developing this kind of specific skills capacity could be included in the remit of the proposed Policy Academies. This is totally different from the 'British jobs for British workers' argument, which is based on a discriminatory idea of denying people access to jobs because of their origin of birth.

Six: education tools. Just as literacy and numeracy were crucial to the development of society and the economy in the past, so too are new types of knowledge and skill which will help to produce an all-of-us-first future. Empathy is at the heart of a better society. Being able to understand the feelings of others and to make those feelings part of your decision-making process is an important way to tackle everything from petty crime to corporate abuse, from poverty to war. There are rapidly-developing educational tools which focus on developing strong empathetic skills and these can be used with all age groups. They help to make better collective decisions, encourage ethical personal actions and reduce violence and anger. Even more established are the practices of conflict resolution which have been developed to help people find ways out of disagreement and to resolve intractable differences, and these should be in much more widespread use.

And what literacy and numeracy were to Scotland's past, so design education is to Scotland's future. If we are to have a design-led future (from smart specialisation in the economy to innovation in how public organisations run) then we need a generation of Scots steeped in the practices and skills of design. Developing a world-class design education curriculum for Scotland might be one of the most important investments Scotland could make.

Seven: information tools. Information and data is already crucial to modern life and will only become more important. The battle will be about the difference between 'me-first information' (secret information used by private interests to make money at the expense of competitors) and 'common information' (public information available to all to help us all create a better society and economy). There is a strong case for proposing a Policy Academy that focuses on information and data and how it should be used to improve lives. The drive to make all information more freely available should include continuing the substantial strengthening of freedom of information laws—knowledge of what is done in the commons (including all government and state activity) should be common information. The recent horrific allegations of historic child abuse do not suggest that the private state and its addiction to secrecy is in the public interest and make an unarguable case for greater transparency. This includes making all government data publicly auditable through open source, preventing UK Government spy agencies and criminal organisations from secretly accessing the information of MSPs and constituents. But public information includes the media and we need new tools to support and sustain a more diverse media to ensure that people have balanced access to views and information.

Eight: community-building tools. It is not enough that we live as atomised individual consumers—community is important to our wellbeing. There are tools we can use to strengthen communities. First we must invest in local facilities, helping communities to become vibrant and bring people together (play parks, town halls, libraries, nurseries). Then we must give people control over their own communities by putting in place real community democracy. We must use the tools being developed in approaches such as Asset-Based Community Development which help communities to regenerate themselves by controlling their own assets and resources. But there are national 'communities of interest' too: these should be supported and activism encouraged, perhaps through an activism fund which helps people to get involved in campaigning and action.

Nine: equality tools. In this respect, people considering Scotland's immediate future have to be honest—if you were to list the key policy tools you would want to use to improve social and economic equality, you'd almost certainly start with macroeconomic and monetary policy, wage policy and regulatory powers, all tax and welfare powers, and control over industrial democracy laws. Scotland will not have access to these tools and that must be recognised. Indeed, many parts of this book are attempts to find solutions despite the lack of really powerful equality tools, either through 'work-arounds' or by emphasising alternative approaches. This means that the focus has to be on investment, collective provision, economic intervention, universalism, and education.

Ten: measurement tools. We need to be able to judge whether we are succeeding or failing in moving towards an all-of-us-first future, which means we need ways to measure progress. Excessively detailed performance indicators both skew people's behaviours (making them manage not the service they are running but rather the performance indicators that have been set) and make it very difficult for ordinary people to understand what is going in. On the other hand, having only one or two headline indicators (GDP and unemployment) is not enough to give a balanced picture. To get that more balanced picture a limited number of new national indicators (for example living standards, quality of national health, wellbeing, wealth inequality, and carbon emissions) should be added. This would create a 'dashboard' of major indicators and these should be issued at the same time to help us better understand how well we are performing.

So we have the tools with which to address our tasks. What we now need is a programme of ideas for what actions will best get those tasks done. That is what the remainder of this book aims to do.

But before moving on, let's look at a couple of approaches and attitudes that will prove invaluable. The first might be called 'look, learn, redesign'. Scotland is clearly not the first nation which has sought to become a better society. So Scotland must always look outwards to see what has been tried, what has worked, and how it was done. There are many nations which have achieved better outcomes than Scotland. We must benchmark ourselves against what they have achieved. And crucially, where we look for our ideas cannot be limited to a straight line running between London and Washington. We can learn much from the Nordic social democracies on welfare and the economy, from Spain on cooperatives, from Germany on a manufacturing economy, from Singapore on open intellectual property rights, from Brazil on participatory democracy and from many, many other places around the world.

Looking and learning is, however, only the start. The things that happened in other countries happened at different times, in different ways, and within different contexts. We can't just 'photocopy' a good idea from somewhere else and imagine it will work 'off the shelf' if only we do exactly the same thing in Scotland. Rather we must take the idea and the learning, and use it to redesign the policies in the context of Scotland now.

We might well start by learning from the Hippocratic oath (the oath doctors take before qualifying). At the heart of that oath is the simple statement 'first, do no harm'. This would be a wonderful starting point to adopt for policy development. Me-first politics is often heard to say variations of the quote attributed to an American military officer in Vietnam - "to save the village we had to destroy it". So to save the poor we must hurt the poor, or to save manufacturing we have to pursue policies that harm manufacturing, to spread wealth we must concentrate wealth, and so on. We are then often told that the negative outcomes which result are 'side effects'. Except there are no side effects, only effects. If you want to help the poor, don't hurt them. If you want to promote manufacturing, don't pursue policies that harm it. If you want to spread wealth, spread wealth. We cannot create a better society if we keep making it worse in the process. Nowhere is this more true than in the fields of climate change and environmental degradation and economic equality, where we keep doing harm while promising to make things better at an unspecified point in the future. It's just making things worse. The cry of 'I want to do the right thing, but not right now' is how we fail to make things better. So in everything we do, we must make things better and in nothing we do should we make things worse.

And the key is indeed 'everything'. Me-first politics is obsessed with 'magic button' politics, the idea that there is one magic button that if we just keep pressing that, everything will be OK. These magic buttons are depressingly familiar: cut tax (especially for the rich), deregulate so business has fewer social responsibilities, inflate house prices, keep inflation low, and so on. This stems from the belief in let-them-do-as-they-please politics, that war of all against all from which the public is supposed to stand aside. That it hasn't worked is hardly surprising—no matter how much they press the 'cut tax' button, very little of the wealth this hands to the rich seems to trickle down to everyone else, and the easier and easier life is made for corporations the more exploitative they appear to become.

If, by comparison, you take a design-led approach then you will immediately realise that everything you do has multiple consequences and anything you want to achieve will be influenced by many factors. If there was a magic button which stopped crime or made us all healthy, someone would have pressed it. In fact, crime and ill-health are consequences of lots of overlapping and interacting factors and unless we engage with all of those factors, we won't be able to fix the problem. Again and again in this book you will see how solutions to big problems are found in almost everything we do. If we do not embrace this complexity and design for holistic change, we will fail.

The only thing that matters is everything we do.

Chapter Three
Defining the commons

The commons has always existed. It is the space where the individual, the private, and the divided give way to community, the public, and the collective. In early societies, most things were in the commons as small communities shared resources and workload to survive. Gradually, as the feudal era took hold and much of the land became private property, still common grazing rights and a common access to land was a constant part of life. With the advent of democracy even the political power in a society was brought into the commons (in theory at least). Over more recent history the commons has grown and shrunk. After 1945 the establishment of the NHS, investment in municipal housing, public amenities such as libraries and public spaces, the nationalising of big industry, and the creation of the welfare state meant that the commons had never been so big. After 1979, the commons came under continued attack with more and more being taken out of the collective realm and placed into the private—usually at great loss to the collective.

Meanwhile the state has existed for thousands of years in many different forms, from kingdoms to empires to nations. The state is, in many ways, an element of the commons. After all, it sets laws and taxes that are common to us all, manages collective resources, and defends the territory in which people live from outside aggression. In the era of kings, the commons (both the land and the people who made it up) was largely the personal property of a monarch, a resource to do with as he pleased. In theory the arrival of mass democracy meant the state was brought fairly and squarely into the commons. In theory we control the state. In practice, however, the state continued (and continues to this day) to maintain large parts of its activity outside the realm not only of democracy but of our knowledge. As a string of scandals in recent years has shown, in fact much of the state continues to operate outside of meaningful democratic oversight, never mind direct democratic control. Hence we have police, security services, senior civil servants and government ministers conspiring to cover up crimes and illegality, not for the common good but for their own benefit.

But at any time we want, we can genuinely take the state fully into the commons. The modern democratic state should, after all, be nothing more than an agreement between its citizens, and if we agree between us that the state must always be under our supervision and always act in our interests, then we can make that happen. Surely the era of 'high-born' people telling us that there are things that are just too complicated for us to understand or too important for us to know about has come to an end? Surely decision-making that marginalises the poor or women or the young is not real democratic decision-making? Surely this really is the era of the full, open, democratic commons?

So what makes up the commons? First of all we have governments and the laws they create. These set out the framework of how the commons will operate (what is legal, what is illegal, by what rules will we behave and so on) and define carefully where the private realm ends and the common realm begins—and vice versa. Government is not only a part of the commons, it is very explicitly chosen by the commons to reflect what the commons wants (again, in theory at least).

Tax is then a crucial part of the commons. Taxes are a 'collective fund' that we authorise government to collect on our behalf to create the resources to invest in our collective good. Me-first politics want us to believe that taxes are a bad thing done 'to' us. In fact they are an incredibly efficient way of saving us money and making us more prosperous by doing things in bulk (private healthcare is massively more expensive than a national health service) and investing in things the market won't (the private sector won't, on its own, pay for roads or schools or police).

It is these areas where we identify collective common need which are best met with collective common action. Some of these are simply not in dispute—even the most extreme of the me-first politicians accept that national defence, policing, core transport infrastructure, refuse collection, the fire service and the criminal justice system are collective responsibilities. There are other areas which the vast majority of people recognise as being part of the commons: education, health, postal service, at least a basic welfare state, social work, regulation, environmental protection, and so on. As much as they would like to, me-first politicians will never persuade people that these should be matters of the private realm. So instead they claim that they should be paid for at least in part collectively, but that private companies should deliver them on a profit-making basis. And common provision of infrastructure and services is not only limited to the national: your local library, your local park, museums and visitor attractions, and many other threads that make up the fabric of our lives are part of those commons.

There may be some debate about some of what is in the commons (many people have become very used to privatised phone and broadband services and don't realise that these were once core national functions which would almost certainly be much better planned and delivered if they were still part of the commons). But we should define this area of collective public service carefully and protect it from exploitation by private profit.

There are then areas which are generally recognised not to be a part of the commons but over which the commons has the right to have influence. So for example few people would call for the full nationalisation of food production and distribution, but most people would react to a crisis in the availability of food by asking what the government had done to protect the interests of citizens. The same is true of areas such as banking and media, which are so important to life that while we may not want them to be run by the commons, we definitely want common action to make sure they are operating at least vaguely in our interests. Which is why we regulate via the commons and why we make common interventions in these areas.

The next area which we all recognise as the commons is common space. We expect to be able to move freely around towns and cities, around the country, between our homes, to places of great historical significance, or great natural beauty. We even expect—subject to respectful behaviour—to be able to move around private land. We also expect a say over the development of space that impacts on our lives through the planning process. So the skyline of our cities is part of our common realm as well as the green land and countryside that we may not own but we do not believe private owners have the right to destroy unilaterally. Now we must shake off years of domination by an out-of-control land and property development industry, recognise that this common space really is our common space, and be much firmer in making sure that it is managed and developed not in the interests of fast profit, but in our common interest. A local park or our village hall is not something that should be taken away from us just because a developer really, really wants it.

Finally, ideas and knowledge are (with limitations) part of the commons too. We are well into the age of 'big data'. In this era we have seen leaps forward in technology and how people use it. We can use the enormous amounts of data being captured to improve our lives (for example by better understanding the causes of ill health). But it can also be used to make our lives worse, by handing our information over to people so they can manipulate us, monitor us, and manage us. The 'ideas and data commons' is an exciting place. By comparison, (mainly) young people are creating international shared networks where you can get free software, free designs for advanced computer equipment, off-the-peg architectural drawings, and much more. We are on the cusp of an exciting new era where we have the capacity to create exciting new ideas, technologies, and software based not on corporations patenting every little bit of their work (in case anyone else benefits), but rather on people sharing every little bit of their work precisely so other people benefit. After all, these people will probably have created their work out of bits and pieces that others shared with them, an accumulated knowledge, much of which was borne not out of the private sector, but by the state through universities and research funding in public services and defence.

So there is a commons of ideas and knowledge out there and we should make sure that when Scotland legislates on 'digital rights', data management, and how it acts over intellectual property it creates virtuous, shared commons and not an exploitative, private realm in which only corporations benefit from data which should belong to us all.

Another essential area of the commons of knowledge and ideas is that everything that is done in and by the commons (with a very few exceptions) is quite literally common knowledge and that we have a complete right to know. Many people believe that we now know most of what the state does. They are wrong. The secret state remains very large and almost unmonitored—from 'commercial confidentiality' in procurement that means we never really know how contracts were awarded, to the security services now shown to be spying on elected politicians. From the appalling revelations about child abuse from the 1970s and 1980s, to the police infiltration of legitimate, peaceful organisations in the 1990s, to the continuing secrecy about police misconduct to this day; we have every reason to demand that being kept in the dark 'for our own good' is no longer acceptable. We need an end to secrecy: it is time for us to be able to decide what is for our own good.

So this is the commons: the governments we elect, the entire state apparatus they govern, the laws that define our society, the tax we raise to invest in our commons, the public services and infrastructure provided, the right to regulate and intervene for our collective good, the space in which we live our lives, and the ideas, knowledge and data which are created by us collectively. We must no longer see 'the state' as something separate from us which can do things to us (and often decide to hide these things from us). We must recognise that all of these things are the commons and that we—citizens—own and govern that commons.

Once we do, we can set out clear principles for how we go about managing that commons. By definition, the commons is a space that is supposed to put 'all of us first'. It is a space for collective action for collective benefit. Over recent decades the sense that certain private interests have privileged access to the commons and that they have used this access to make the commons work for them and not for us has decreased our trust in the commons. And ironically, that reduced trust has generally suited them—at least so long as we shrugged and said to ourselves 'well of course the banks and the government are up to their necks in it'. But now there are very clear signs that this trust has broken down, so much so that there is a strong public demand to clean up politics and government. This is happening all over the world, but it is particularly visible in Scotland. So that simple principle must be re-established—of the people, by the people, for the people. And not just some of the people.

The commons should vigorously guard the principle of universalism. That simple concept—from each according to ability, to each according to need—is perhaps the highest degree of civilisation we have reached. Not by birth, not by wealth, but by right. Your right to be educated, to be treated when you're ill, to be protected by a police force—all of it. Me-first politics is constantly trying to persuade us that this is an out-dated idea, or unfair, or inefficient. Why should the poor pay for the healthcare of the rich? Well, they don't. We all pay tax according to what we can afford (or at least we should) and then we use that tax to create the services that we all need. We all then get free access to those services. This universal approach is incredibly efficient and effective, and has been shown to be so over and over again. By making it a universal right, there is no shame in going for free medical treatment and we all have a collective desire to make that treatment as good as it can be. Universalism is not meant to be 'progressive' (linked to wealth) in its delivery, it's meant to be excellent, efficient, and effective in its delivery. It's meant to be progressive in how we pay for it.

But above all, it works—and it works incredibly well. If you include everyone, everyone is lifted up. But those most in need are lifted up much more than those who are already affluent. Nothing has done more to equalise the quality of life for everyone than universalism, and absolutely nothing has done more to take away the terrible privations faced by the poorest (not least the stigma of charity) than universalism. It must be protected at all costs.

Another principle is that the commons is defined by the investment we make into it. Investment is at the very heart of the idea of a politics that puts all of us first. To understand why this is so, it helps to think about the difference between investment and speculation. Investment means to expend time and effort now in the belief that it will make the future better. Speculation means to use money to try and make more money. The first improves things for all, the second improves things for those who have lots of money—but at the expense of others. Me-first politics has led us to believe that we can speculate our way to a better society through casino banks, dodgy property deals, and the endless expansion of retail. At the same time it has allowed the fabric of our society to deteriorate from lack of investment (from privatised rail services to the closure of public libraries). Despite that flawed 'let them do as they please' logic, the future does not get better without investment. We must accept that just as that post-war generation made a massive investment in itself (which we continue to benefit from to this day), so must we invest in our future so our children continue to benefit.

Me-first has used the commons to speculate and create wealth for the few. It is time to invest in the commons.

All of this should be driven by the concept of social security. The economy that has developed in Britain thrives on insecurity. The fear that life without work is so hard forces people to accept any conditions offered to them: low pay, zero-hours contracts, unsociable working hours, or demeaning work. This certainly suits a particular kind of employer (i.e. those that create low-pay, low-quality, and anti-social jobs), but it does not suit us collectively. It encourages precisely the wrong kind of economy, creates all kinds of health and social problems, and perhaps above all it establishes anxiety as a political tool. Anxiety should simply never be used as a political tool—it's a cruel and inhumane way to run a society in an era of plenty. We should want to build a society based on high-quality, high-value work and collective wellbeing and solidarity. That needs our citizens to be secure, not anxious. Social security provides people with the knowledge that come what may (unless they break the law), they will be okay; that they and their family will not be hungry, cold, homeless or unable to participate in society. Social security is a combination of many factors (housing, employment, welfare, energy prices, cost of living and so on). This idea—that a citizen should feel secure in their future and should be able to build from that— must be integrated into everything we do in the commons.

In all of this, we must also recognise that while we are all part of a society that should put all of us first, that does not mean that we will all believe the same things, feel the same way, or have the same views. Me-first politics often implies that the only alternative to its beloved war of all against all is some sort of oppressive, Orwellian state imposing a single view on everyone with personal freedom sacrificed to the needs of the state. This is beyond silly. Putting all of us first also means protecting our rights to hold the beliefs we hold. A Common Weal future can only be achieved if it is built on pluralism, diversity, and democracy. We identify what we have in common and we build on that—but we also recognise what makes us different and we respect and protect that right to be different.

This rights-focussed approach to understanding what it should mean to be a citizen is crucial. The me-first media has for years run a campaign suggesting that human rights are only for 'bad people'. This is unsurprising. After all, if you want a war of all against all, the last thing you want is for your combatants to have the protection of rights. Human rights are a statement of the morality we expect to underpin our society. It is a first step in outlining what we mean by 'common decency'. But common decency is also about more than just rights; it is a statement of values. At the heart of those values is empathy: the ability to recognise and understand what others feel. So much of what has gone wrong with the global economy can be seen precisely as a failure to recognise and value what others suffer as a result of the actions of large, powerful players (whether that be poverty, environmental degradation, global warming, ill-health, war, violence or death).

We live in the freest society in history. That freedom—that right to be different, to hold values and beliefs important to you, whether they are shared by others or not—is the result of centuries of struggle. The liberal belief in the right to that freedom is very much part of our common weal. But it has an essential counterpart: the right to our own freedom and wellbeing is not an excuse to ignore the freedom and the wellbeing of others. The essential price for our freedom is that we understand that it cannot come at the expense of someone else's; if it does then it can only be a matter of time before it is our own freedom that comes second. Common decency understands that our own wellbeing is inextricably linked to the wellbeing of those around us.

And then it is only left for us to be vigilant; to make sure that our commons is used for us and not to make us poorer or weaker. Privatisation, consultancy culture, the capture of politics by financial industries, one-sided trade agreements, the influence of corporate lobbying—all of these are attempts to use the commons as a means of extracting wealth from citizens for the benefit not of citizens, but of commercial interests. This is the opposite of what the commons is for and it must be resisted.

If we can properly understand the public realm around us as the commons, and understand that we don't just live in it, we own it, then we can better understand how best to protect and improve our commons and how to use it to make our lives better. The outcome of getting this right by following the principles above is greater efficiency, greater effectiveness, greater justice and fairness, more equality, and a reinvigorated sense of citizenship and community. If we give up on the commons, we really do leave ourselves at the mercy of that war of all against all. And we'll almost all lose.

Chapter Four
To build more we must share more

The economy is, at heart, a system of social provisioning. Which simply means that it is a system which should produce the things society needs and distribute them to the people who need them—and do so in a way which ensures that it will continue to be able to produce these things in the future. Simple really. If you accept this definition of the economy then it becomes relatively easy to understand if your economy is working. Are the things that currently exist and that we need (food, clothing, shelter, entertainment, and so on) being produced effectively and efficiently? Is the production model successfully getting these products to members of society? Are there things that don't yet exist but that we need (such as new medicines or technologies which improve our lives)? Is the economy innovating and creating these new things? Are these being successfully distributed to the people who need them?

There is no part of our society which has been so fully captured by the religion of 'me first' than the economy. The concept of the economy as a system of social provisioning has been entirely transformed into the concept of the economy as a system of personal enrichment. To justify this transformation, me-first economists have claimed that it is personal enrichment that drives the whole system. That claim is based on a trick of language—the definition of the word 'profit'.

There is no doubt that profit is an important part of the economy. Whether you're me-first or all-of-us-first just depends on what you mean by profit. For those who believe that the economy is a system of social provisioning, profit is essential because it is that profit that ensures the future ability to continue to create the goods and services we need. In this view, an enterprise generates profit for reinvestment. That investment ensures sustainability, innovation, and improvement. The me-first version of profit is different. They believe that profit is a personal reward for those who make the system work (and they are not the people who do the work but rather those who own the enterprise). This theory suggests that the more profit an owner can make, the harder they will work. The 'profit motive' is not to reinvest to strengthen the enterprise but to incentivise rich people to keep doing more of the same.

For over 40 years the profit-as-reward view of the economy has dominated. And as we can see through rising inequality, the continued existence of poverty, the wasteful nature of markets, the environmental harm being done, the low productivity, the lack of investment, the weak innovation, and the overall instability of the system; that model of the economy has failed. Remember the me-first brigade believe nothing more wholeheartedly than that the economy is above and beyond society, that it is outwith the democratic realm, that it belongs to 'wealth creators', and that a democratic government has no right to intervene. Except that every time the 'wealth creators' (who should very often be more accurately described as wealth extractors) screw up the economy, they expect the commons to chip in and save them. So what is it me-firsters; 'let us do as we please' or 'please bail us out'?

It is time to take this decision out of their hands, since it is based on a blatantly incorrect assumption. The economy is not above and beyond society. Rather the economy is there to serve society and nothing else. It is a system which we support to an enormous degree through our common investment. It is us who educate the workforce, it is us who build the roads so goods can get to market, it is us who provide a police force to protect assets, it is us who build a telecommunication system. Advocates of me-first claim that it's the owners of enterprises who 'create wealth'. But it isn't. It's the people who work in enterprises that create wealth through their work (the owner of a factory with no-one to work in it creates no wealth; a factory of workers with no owner manages to create wealth just fine on their own—they're called cooperatives). And perhaps most fundamentally of all, we create the wealth because it is us who buys the goods and services produced.

Wealth is not created by individuals, it is created by a society. The economy does not serve those individuals, it serves society—or at least it should. That should be our aim: to create a social economy. That economy should support society by strengthening it, support our environment by protecting it, support our democracy by being embedded in it, support our communities by being part of them, support our workers by treating them with respect. And in truth, that is how much of our economy behaves. Despite all the tall tales told by advocates of me-first, most of our indigenous businesses are rooted in our communities. They're not perfect (for example, few are unionised). But much more than multinational corporations, they want to be good members of that community, to be respected by that community. They look their workforce in the eyes every day and generally do not spend their time trying to reduce the pay and conditions of their employees. They want to reinvest, to build for the future. They range from the small corner shop to the large independent manufacturing business. And mostly they want to take a long-term view. After all, they will still be reliant on their business to survive next year and the year after that.

And yet they are not the part of our economy for which economic policy is designed. They are told that the only role of government is to create a 'level playing-field'. Then in that war of all against all they are expected to fight off the power of giant corporations and big banks which are granted privileged access to that 'level playing field'. Make no mistake, the me-first economy has been just about as bad for independent businesses as it has been for low wage workers.

This has had serious knock-on effects. Big corporations are now as much financial institutions as they are productive enterprises. They claim to be compelled by law to create the highest profit possible for their shareholders at all times. So investment is skewed to produce short-term profits, which generally means that investments are speculative. And the business model is built on trying to extract the most profit out of their customers in the shortest possible period of time. That generally means paying employees and suppliers as little as possible and taking as much money from their customers as they can (either by inflating prices as in the housing market, or by increasing the volume of sales by aggressive advertising as in the retail sector).

These perverse incentives have created a low-pay, low-skill, low-productivity, low-innovation, low-investment, short-term, high-profit-extracting economy. This has reduced pay, increased inequality, reduced manufacturing, overheated consumption, made housing unaffordable for many, harmed the environment and led to constant instability. This is the opposite of a social economy. We should start again and rethink our strategy for the economy.

First of all, as an advanced economy with very high levels of education we should be focussing our efforts on stimulating a high-pay economy. Indeed we should probably go further and actively discourage a low-pay economy. As was discussed in chapter one, it is an economy creating high-pay jobs which kicks off the loop that builds the good society—productive economy, high pay, prosperous citizens, strong public finances, high investment into the commons, good social infrastructure, high social cohesion, and so on.

High pay jobs are good for all of us. If people have higher wages then they consume in different ways. Rather than buying poor-quality, cheap, imported goods they buy high-quality, locally produced goods (no-one in high-pay Norway buys cheap, processed bread but rather high-quality freshly baked bread which is often artisanal and produced by a local baker). This again creates a virtuous loop as high-quality local producers create more high-pay jobs and then those prosperous employees in turn create more high-pay jobs through their spending habits. In Britain we've created the worst deal possible, which goes something like 'here's a pitifully low wage—but to make up for it here are some rubbish but incredibly cheap sausages made with horse meat we won't tell you about and other unspeakable ingredients; enjoy'. It is hard to overstate how bad a deal it is; for our health, for our prosperity, for our wellbeing, for our economy, and for the environment. It is essential that we understand just how much we would all benefit from paying more for things like food, clothes, and furniture—so long as it is matched by rising wages. We need to break the destructive low-pay, low-quality life loop and replace it with the high-pay, high-quality life loop which would greatly improve, well, everything.

But how do we do that? The answer is in productivity. If you increase wages without increasing productivity it runs the risk of creating inflation and making the economy constantly less efficient and so less competitive. High pay for bad jobs is not the aim. But if you increase wages as a result of increased productivity, it will not affect inflation. And because that productivity would be based on investment in high skills and innovation, it produces a more specialised economy which becomes competitive not on the basis of low cost but on quality. All jobs can be better and better jobs drive better pay.

So how do we improve productivity? Productivity is simply how much value the economy creates for each hour worked. It is possible to increase productivity by making employees work harder or for less money, but that is most certainly not the kind of productivity which creates a high-wage workforce. Rather it is by improving the value added by the economy that we get the right kind of productivity. And to understand how to do that, simply think about what 'added value' is.

If you buy goods cheaply from abroad, import them, mark up the price and then sell them more expensively to your customers you will make a profit. But that profit will come from the mark-up: from taking more out of your customers' pockets than you paid for the goods. But they're the same goods; the total value stayed the same, only the price changed. It requires no skill, only the use of money to buy and mark up the goods. So the profit comes not from labour but from already having money. And you will make very little investment—all you need is a glorified shed in an out-of-town shopping complex. And you will require very few skills, only someone to put the goods on the shelves. And since it's all so profitable and easy, you have very little incentive to innovate. So you will pay very little to your staff who are unskilled and not being asked to innovate. And to be competitive, you will keep your margins low and your turnover high. So you will be fundamentally unproductive, because you won't produce anything.

If rather than buying a cheap piece of clothing from China and selling it a bit more expensively you actually make a piece of clothing, the economics are entirely different. This time you buy raw materials and transform them (and importantly, smaller scale production tends to buy more materials from within its own economy, cascading the benefits of productivity). What you finish with (a completed garment) is substantively different than what you began with (some cloth). And it is worth much more than what you began with. That is real added value, and you have added the value through your skill. So now you get the value from skill which means you pay for that skill. This makes wages higher because they're not based on 'squeezing the margins' (trying to cut as many costs as you can) but on 'investing in skill'. And your work is highly productive.

Put simply, this is why it is essential that Scotland rebalances its economy away from sectors of the economy which are basically wealth-extracting (which make their profit from customers by squeezing the margins, and which do not reinvest those profits in the economy but rather export them overseas to shareholders) to ones which are genuinely wealth-creating. Or at minimum they should be wealth-retaining (of course we need retail, but the more of the retail sector which is smaller and independent, the more of our collective wealth stays within our collective economy). We need much more manufacturing, a high-skill service sector, and a much more diverse profile of enterprise ownership. And since another important route to productivity is through technology (being able to do things better), high investment is also key.

To do this we need to take a more mutual and more engaged approach to the economy. 'Let them do as they please' is a very bad philosophy for creating a diverse, productive, and innovative economy. Rather we must focus on setting the right goals and creating the right approaches to achieve them. Key among these is to replace 'let them do as they please' economic development strategies with a design-led strategy based on a mutual approach. This will recognise that of course businesses within an industry sector will compete against each other, but they also have an enormous number of interests in common. So economic policy should design the best possible environment which will enable all the players in an industry sector to be as effective as they can. Only once the best possible environment is created should the collective interest say 'that's far enough now, time for you to find your own way'. This mutual approach will not produce 'magic button' solutions but will rather produce a detailed and interconnected programme covering everything from education to infrastructure to export support to supply chain resilience.

And importantly, because there are no magic buttons, the economic strategy which will emerge will be distinct and tailored to each sector of the economy. This is particularly true because of the fragmented nature of the British economy which is typified by giant corporation, lots of very small businesses, few medium-sized businesses, and weak supply chains. Some of our domestic economy really is at the cutting edge of the world economy, but some of it is plodding along in exactly the same way it has for decades. This is a very big mistake. If we look at really successful economies they do not just transform and innovate in their high-tech and sunrise industries, but in all parts of their economy. They improve construction technologies and build houses in new ways, they change the techniques of agricultural production, they turn apparently old-fashioned industries into cutting edge ones (such as how the Nordic countries transformed their timber industry into one of the world's most innovative advanced material industries).

Recent economic development strategies in Scotland have always had a tension between the fear that a few macroeconomic measures are not enough but that 'picking winners' (picking industry sectors in which to intervene) is too risky. The answer is to do neither. Rather than economic development professionals doing policy 'to' sectors of the economy, structures should be created which enable sectors of the economy to come together and devise their own strategies. It is by harnessing the knowledge and innovative potential of enterprises, workers, researchers, educators, and others working together to devise the best possible plan, that we will create better enterprises in all parts of the economy. Indeed we should follow a motto—'no sector left behind': no part of our economy too boring, routine, or old-fashioned to ignore its potential for innovation, change, and growth.

It will take time. Britain has a very uneven level of economic development and so it will take some sectors longer than others to become the best versions of what they could be. But once that is achieved we will also gain the benefits of interconnectedness. Another mistake made by me-first economics is to see an economy as a series of individual enterprises. It isn't, it's a system of interconnected enterprises. The aim is that the maximum number of supply chain enterprises (providing goods and services to other enterprises) can be built up and sustained within the same economy as the enterprises they supply. This needs as many enterprises as possible to be at the same level of development, to be equally advanced, and able to talk and trade with each other on equal terms. Because of Britain's uneven economic development, we seldom have consistent supply chains at a consistent level of sophistication and in many cases we just have no supply chain at all. This will require some patience. It will require many parts of the economy to 'grow up together', and it may require us to support and stimulate parts of the economy that appear to be missing or particularly weak. When we get there, the interconnectedness will also include colleges, universities, research institutes, and many other partners, all able to work together as equals. But a 'let them do as they please' approach will not only fail to achieve this, it will continue to push us in the opposite direction as smaller domestic supply chain companies are pushed out of business by global corporate competitors using their power to influence markets so that smaller competitors can't compete.

And the key to producing a robust, resilient, productive, and innovative enterprise? Workers. In the kind of economy Scotland should aim to create it is high-skill workers and not 'asset sweating' or 'squeezing the margins' that generate success. We have already seen how skill creates added value and how added value creates prosperity and wellbeing. But it is also through the knowledge of workers that the economy is best able to innovate. In successful economies, it is employee innovation which drives many advances, not consultants or even scientists in laboratories. It is the driver who realises that doing the deliveries in a different order would be much more efficient, the factory worker who realises that if the conveyor belt was going in a different direction more people could work at it, or the garment worker who thinks of trying a different cloth than the one that was 'always used'.

But British workers are not less intelligent or educated than those in economies with high rates of employee innovation—so what's the difference? Above all, it is the governance of enterprises which hampers innovation in Britain. It is when there are employee representatives on company boards and good and effective mutual shop-floor governance that employees have both the incentive and the mechanism for driving change. If employees share in the responsibility of running companies then they will work to make those companies great. If their work is treated like another disposable material by managers, they will respond in kind. Mutual governance is a win-win for all concerned.

It also plays a part in changing the ethos of the economy. Britain is plagued by 'entrepreneur porn' with television and the media fetishising get-rich-quick schemes and flashy marketing approaches to building a business. The finance pages and the bars of the City of London idolise mergers and acquisitions, buy-outs and restructuring, battles for equity control and the financial returns from downsizing and financial innovation. A business no longer makes a thing, a thing makes a business. It's your patent or your business model that matters and hopefully someone will come along and buy your patent or your business model. Then you can invest the money in property like just about everyone else in Britain who got rich over the last 30 years. This 'saw tooth' economy (building up company value not to sustain it but to sell it and then start again) is enormously damaging to society. The finance and business pages celebrate when a 'Scottish entrepreneur' becomes a millionaire by selling his or her company. What we are really celebrating is the loss of all the jobs, all the supply chain, all the skills and experience—and the future growth potential.

Instead we need a 'circular' economy in which business leaders are in it for the long term, want to build up companies which are effective and respected, want to be part of their community, and who would see an equity sale as a failure. This is the German Mittelstand model (Mittelstand means 'medium-sized' and refers to often family-owned businesses which are big producers of often well-known household goods, pay high wages and innovate, and retain a long-term commitment to their ownership, their community, their workers, and their supply chain). These businesses do not seek to take out profit as quickly as possible so managers can buy luxury goods and they certainly do not build themselves up to sell themselves to the highest bidder. A different ethos exists and it is a much more mutual ethos which is focussed on real enterprise, not personal enrichment or celebrity status. And because they involve workers closely in all aspects of management these businesses really are anchored in their community and their economy.

This achieves two additional things. First, it creates a more responsible economy. After all, when you plan to be rooted in a place for many decades to come you have a strong incentive not to be a bad neighbour, not to pollute, not to degrade the environment, not to short-change workers, not to undermine the strength of the local community, not to allow massive income disparity across the workforce, to respect gender and other equalities in the workforce, not to abuse migrant labour and so many other of the attitudes that should underpin an ethical and responsible economy. Because if an economy is part of society and must serve society then it should be the job of the commons to make sure that this is what the economy is really doing. Ideally that should be achieved by creating the incentives to build an economy with the right ethos and the right structures to enable it properly to serve society. But getting there may also require more active regulation and more assertive interventions to prevent negative behaviours, not least in terms of low-pay employment, gender equality, and environmental protection.

The second thing it will start to achieve is to emphasise that the socially useful part of the economy is there to produce socially useful goods and services. The economic model that we have emphasises economic approaches which are about low margins and high turnovers so that we constantly produce things that no-one really wants. And then we spend an inordinate amount of resource using sophisticated advertising and marketing techniques to make people buy the goods and services—but in the certain knowledge that they will not be buying these things next year when an entirely different range of goods and services no-one wants will be saturation-marketed at us. This is the mechanism by which corporations seek to squeeze more and more income out of our pockets into theirs; not through increasing utility (making things more useful) but by increasing futility (the speed at which we dispose of the last pointless thing we bought). This is an economic problem that has infected all parts of society and should be addressed in part by emphasising an economy which is productive, not extractive.

This is the economy Scotland should have: productive by creating high-pay jobs and a more equal distribution of resources and income, which in turn increases productivity and strengthens domestic markets (which make up about 70 per cent of the economy). This would be highly innovative and would focus on 'smart specialisation' (working out what specific things we do well and doing them very well indeed) and not equity sales, saturation marketing of consumer goods, and domination of almost all parts of the economy by corporations. It would have many more forms of ownership including social enterprises and cooperatives. It would be interconnected and at a consistent level of development. It would be ethical and responsible, and would treat men and women equally and without the gender segregation of work which results in so many women working in low-pay sectors. And we will have gotten there by adopting mutual approaches to development.

Unfortunately, Scotland does not have anything like the powers it needs to achieve this fully. Seeking to achieve this economy will have to take place against the use of macroeconomic, monetary, regulatory, pay, welfare, and industrial democracy powers which look certain to be driven in the opposite direction by the UK Government. But there are still a wide range of powers and interventions that can be used and made. We need to be active in using them and to be guided by this vision in getting there.

It's known as having an industrial policy.

Chapter Five
Design for life

Look around you. Look at your house, your street, your neighbourhood, your town centre, the place where you work, the places you shop. Think about how you spend your time, the time you have with friends and family, the time you have to yourself, the time you spend at work, the time you spend doing 'things'. Consider the way you spend your money, what you spend it on, what you do with the things you spend it on. Ask yourself why you live where you live, why you work where you work, why you buy what you buy. What do you do? How do you enjoy yourself? Now think back. What did you think you were going to do? How did you want to live? Is this it? Focus on one big question:

How much of this did you choose and how much of this 'just happened'?

In truth you probably didn't actively choose much of it. At some point you just noticed that you seemed to be working an awful lot of hours but then each time you thought about doing something about it you realised that you're trapped by a mortgage. In truth, you probably quite often find yourself browsing in shops and you're not completely sure why (you didn't come out of the house wanting the things being sold). You probably really did want to learn joinery as a hobby, or dressmaking, or amateur dramatics. You probably did enjoy the things you thought you were going to do (climb a hill, potter in the garden, write that novel). You may tell yourself that these were all childish notions that you've outgrown since you became 'an adult' with 'responsibilities'. But you're probably wrong. You would probably get to the top of that hill and you'd probably look out at the vista below you and feel joy. And there is a good chance it would be the kind of deep and moving joy that you just don't get from buying another t-shirt. How did you get here? How did we get here? In truth we didn't get here, we were brought here.

For much of human existence we designed our lives for survival. That is because for much of human life we faced an environment of scarcity; it took a lot of time and effort to produce food, fabric, and houses. We lived in the fear that tomorrow we wouldn't have enough on which to live. But then came the industrial revolution (and agricultural revolutions as well). Suddenly human productivity sky-rocketed and we could produce everything we needed. This was an era of abundance. Our technological development meant that we could easily produce enough of everything for everyone. But that created a problem: if everyone is satisfied, how does industry and commerce continue to grow?

The answer was fairly simple. We had to stop designing life for survival and start designing life for profit. At the turn of the 20th century a group of thinkers concluded that if the industrial revolution had provided people with everything they needed, then there was only one option: to start making people want more and more things. It was called 'manufacturing desire' and it spawned everything from modern advertising and marketing to the contemporary shopping mall. It 'designed for profit' because it converted public spaces (which the Victorians had often created as proud civic spaces) into opportunities to increase commerce. They became privatised (shopping malls take up large parts of our cities but are entirely private spaces with no democracy), saturated with advertising, planned to drive the footfall going through towns into shops, with civic spaces redesigned for the purposes of commercial interests (such as the recent plans to develop George Square in Glasgow not so people can enjoy it during their lunch hour, but so big commercial promotions can have maximum access and space).

Cities have become a competition between giant commercial interests who want to litter the skylines with skyscrapers dedicated to themselves. Towns have been undermined and hollowed out by out-of-town retail parks which aim to get us to spend more and more in big corporate 'superstores' and less and less in small local shops. Shopping malls are carefully designed with no views to the outside world (so we lose our sense of time) and with layouts explicitly designed to disorientate us and encourage us to walk past (and into) ever more shops.

Our lifestyles are shaped not to enhance our lives but to enhance profits. As public amenities like libraries are forced out of our lives, so endless new developments that encourage us to spend money on commercial entertainment proliferate. For many people, playing frisbee with their kids in a public park is becoming a thing of the past (public parks make no-one any money and a cheap frisbee will last you the rest of your life—so no one really wants to make them, promote them, or sell them).

Despite incredible improvements in technology and productivity our working hours are becoming longer, not shorter as they should. We are being pushed to work these extra hours to earn money not so much to improve our lives, but so we have more money for inventive multinational corporations to take from us.

And one of the most effective ways for commerce to take money from us is through 'status anxiety'. The people who realised that 'manufacturing desire' was the key to enabling big business to continue to expand discovered that the best way to manufacture desire was to create anxiety in customers; the fear that by not owning a product they would be seen as failures by their peers. Modern advertising is filled with beautiful, happy, successful, smiley people but they almost all give over the same message: they're only smiling because they have something you don't and if you don't have it not only will you not be happy, but you won't be accepted by these other beautiful, successful people.

The real horror in this is that almost no-one can actually own all these products (not that it would actually make you happy even if you could). So we are made to feel constantly inferior, insecure, like a failure. This anxiety is a part of why we face declining mental health in the developed west; the more we shop in the mistaken belief that it will make us happier, the more we are made to feel unhappy by all the things that surround us that we will never own, all the photographs of models we will never be.

It is one of the most depressing truths about modern commerce: those with the power and the money want us to be unhappy. Why? Because happy people don't shop.

And here's the strange thing: as we have already seen, when you ask people what is important to them, it is financial security, a nice home, good public space, respect at work in a job they enjoy, time with friends and family, their health and happiness, and to be part of a community.

When you ask people what they want from their lives they almost never begin by talking about consumer goods, and yet by designing our lives for profit we all seem to have been placed in a race to acquire more and more of these plastic items which clog up our houses, until we eventually throw them out, often barely used.

Nowhere are our designed-for-profit lives causing us more unhappiness than in our homes. People talk about the housing market and property developers. This is somewhat misleading. If we look at the economy of the property sector what we are really buying are tradable assets and these tradable assets are (unsurprisingly) being managed to maximise profit. The problem is, very few of us will ever be able to profit from our house because it doesn't matter how much its price rises, even if we sell it at a profit we still need somewhere to live. And effectively we will have to buy this new home at a loss because of deliberately inflated housing costs. We don't win. Banks win. And property developers, and property speculators—many of the new houses being built in London are never intended to be occupied, but to be owned as financial assets.

In fact property developers might more truthfully be described as land developers because trading in land is basically what they do. It is land values and planning permission that really makes them money; building houses is only the way they release the profit. And so they build houses with one aim: to extract the maximum amount of money from the land they own. This does not actually mean that they will build as many houses on that land as they can; they will build the number of houses which makes them most money (though the British live in the smallest houses in Europe as a result). And because being able to sell a house as a 'villa with garden' is the most profitable option, they pack houses together but not efficiently joined to each other (as terraces and tenements were), and with all public spaces sacrificed for tiny gardens which inflate the price of the development.

These big housing developments all have pavements, but nowhere to go on them. No parks, no shops, no cafe, no pub, no restaurant, no economy. No community, just a giant grid of families crammed into their postage stamp-sized gardens with nowhere to meet each other. And like the way town and city centres have been developed, there is almost no sense that anyone took a proper overview of it all, just to see if the totality of what they were building was going to be beautiful and life enhancing or ugly and soul destroying. The philosophy of 'let them do as they please' means that people with money can build pretty well whatever they want, wherever they want. If it looks to you like a bit of a horrendous mess, an unplanned jumble of vanity projects, and endless, soulless housing schemes, and if you've ever felt like a bystander with no control over this awful sprawl, you're not alone.

All of this makes us feel isolated, alone, alienated, and without community. It cramps us in small and massively overpriced houses which are built to some of the lowest quality standards in Europe. Towns and even the streets in which we live are designed first for cars, second for people. We are surrounded by the constant drone of fast-moving vehicles. There are many places we simply can't walk to and even if we do, we're surrounded by exhaust fumes and the danger of accidents.

It makes us passive. It makes us buy highly processed food rather than cook. It does nothing to encourage our participation in community and society. We are overweight, unhealthy, and often miserable. Our world is designed for profit and it now sees us not as a community, but as a source of that profit. The way we are corralled and coerced into spending money, they way national success is then measured according to how much we spend, this increasingly makes us seem less like citizens and more like livestock.

We must stop designing for profit. Profit is not wealth. In fact it has been said that there is no wealth but life (the old world 'Weal' in Common Weal can mean both wealth and wellbeing and in fact seeing these as separate and different things is comparatively recent). So we need to start designing for life; as a command. Design! For life!

What would it look like if we did? If you go to Edinburgh you can start to see the difference. Look at some of the peripheral housing estates, the retail parks, the ugly jumble of the financial district. Then look at the beautifully designed symmetry of the New Town, it's character, the balance between regularity and surprise in its architecture, the way it invites you to walk around it, the way it has left space for landscaping, green space. The way it has an economy built in. Edinburgh's New Town was designed for its citizens and for their lives.

We can do that again. We can build houses that make great, efficient use of space, which create community and economy, with amenities and parks, local pubs and cafes and restaurants. We can build them so they are beautiful, with real green space. We can make them places that invite their residents to walk, to explore, and to discover. The houses will be bigger, warmer, better to live in—and much cheaper. They'd be of mixed sizes and types to encourage a diverse environment. They'd be linked via great transport to places of work and bigger civic amenities.

We'd design our society to make it easy and normal for us to participate in our community, in civic life. We'd alter and adapt design techniques in order to develop services which suited all members of society, and not just the white, male-centred population. We'd invest in building life-enhancing infrastructure. We'd encourage the activities which make us feel good about ourselves (learning, hobbies, sports, the arts, travel, activism, community participation) and collectively limit the way that advertising makes us feel bad about ourselves.

We'd plan our spaces for us, not for cars. City centres would be places for people to meet, not places to drive us into shops. We'd build an economy that created higher-quality, longer-lasting goods which we'd value. We'd make quality food an indispensable part of our lives. We'd work fewer hours and our lives would not be dictated by our mortgages (partly because housing would be cheaper and partly because many more of us would choose the option of a brilliant quality public rental house if they were available). We'd see policing and criminal justice not in terms of who we can punish or lash out at, but in terms of what will make our lives better, safer, and more trusting. The big institutions in our society would value our time with our family. We'd stop tolerating being 'farmed' for profit.

We've been trapped by public and private bureaucracies which have almost completely absorbed this mania for managing society based on economic indicators (which is another way of saying 'designed for profit'). They make decisions about our lives based on a belief that the foremost task ahead of us is always to satisfy 'the economy'. We chase after these numbers which are supposed to tell us if we're doing this effectively. When the numbers look 'right' we pat ourselves on the back and conclude that we're making 'progress', no matter what it looks like outside the window. Then again, a dog chasing its tail believes it's making progress too.

If we were designing for life, every time we came to make a decision we'd make that decision not based on whether it is likely to increase or decrease a notional number which is supposed almost magically to lead to economic growth. If we were designing for life we'd use our own minds to decide what was beautiful, what was worthwhile, what would make us happy, what would leave a legacy of dignity and respect.

There is no wealth but life. If we do not learn this lesson and change how we make decisions, we will condemn ourselves to chase our tails forever. And we will sacrifice our happiness in the process.

Part Two

WHAT SHOULD WE DO?

Chapter Six
Building the commons

Before we use the commons to build a great public realm, to create
the best environment for positive economic growth and to improve
people's lives, we need to invest in the commons. That begins with tax.

Tax

We should see tax as fulfilling three basic purposes. First, tax
pays for common services and common infrastructure. Second,
tax redistributes wealth across society, helping to compensate for a
chronically unequal economy. Third, tax helps to influence behaviour
through creating both positive and negative incentives.

There are then three principles that a tax system should be based
on. Firstly it should be progressive and fair. Progressive means that the
amount and rate of tax is linked to the ability of someone to pay that tax;
the more you can afford to pay, the more you pay. This is easy to apply
to income, wealth, and profits but may be different in the case of some
taxes that are used to influence behaviour (such as a tax on products like
tobacco which cause harm, or taxes to encourage better environmental
performance). In these cases the taxes may not be progressive but they
must be seen to be fair, affordable, not punitive, and clearly linked to a
just outcome. And everyone must be treated equally—if corporations
are allowed to use complex accounting deals to avoid paying their tax, it
simply reduces trust in the whole system.

Secondly tax should be effective and efficient. Every loophole written
into tax law not only loses the commons income via evasion, but costs the
commons more to police. As far as possible, taxes should be easy to collect
because they are designed to be simple, consistent, and clearly defined.
However, that does not mean that a tax should be opposed simply
because it is more difficult to collect; evasion and avoidance are no reason
for people to 'get away with it'. Taxes which are designed to influence
behaviour or to create fairness (for example by targeting those who have
used evasion and avoidance) may be more difficult to collect, but they

should still be effective in achieving their aims.

Thirdly, tax should be comprehensible and understood to be fair. It is not enough that taxes are effective or technically fair if those subject to the tax cannot understand why or how the tax has been levied. Tax should always be calculable and citizens must be able to understand how their tax bill is determined and why. This is absolutely essential to allow strong trust in the tax system.

Me-first politics likes to separate tax from its wider context, mainly because it seeks to trade on the perceived unpopularity of tax. In fact, tax is only unpopular when it is not felt to be fair, effective, and comprehensible, or where the investment made with the tax income is seen as wasteful or ineffective. Tax must be contextualised. It should be linked to the positive case of investing in the commons, particularly in its utility to personal needs: if a citizen were to have to replace the services provided by tax from their own pocket, it would cost them many multiples of what they pay in tax for the same thing.

But in turn, any tax strategy must take into account the wider economic context. Scotland suffers from Britain's low-pay culture. Roughly half of the working population earns under £21,000 a year, a third earn under £15,000 and three in five earn less than £25,000. One in five earn between £25,000 and £35,000 and one in five earn over £35,000. Fewer than one in 20 Scots earns over £50,000 and many fewer still earn over £100,000. This data communicates two very substantial problems. The first is that for large proportions of the population, available income is very tight (and this is greatly compounded by Britain's remarkably high housing costs). The three in five people who earn under the average wage of £25,000 simply face limited affordability, and it would be difficult to raise much additional common tax revenue without placing substantial cost pressure on them. This does not mean that some modest additional contribution is impossible (for example if people are asked to pay a bit more in local taxes). But Scotland's income profile means that we would find it very hard to raise substantial income from basic rate income tax alone. This is particularly the case given that income tax makes up only a little more than a quarter of tax income (rising to just over two fifths if the less progressive National Insurance Contributions are included).

The second substantial problem is that there simply aren't enough people paying higher rate taxes to be able to raise enough from them alone to solve investment problems. To reach the 40p tax band you only need to be earning £32,000. If you think of this in the case of it being a single family income, then it becomes clear that the ability to raise more income by raising this rate is much more limited. If you introduce higher bands (for example a higher tax rate at £50,000) you are better able to meet affordability criteria—but in turn you reduce the numbers paying that tax and so reduce the ability to increase income from it. By the time you get to the top band of £150,000, you begin to deal with a small number of people (and you have the added problem that Britain's tax system seems virtually designed for them to avoid tax anyway).

Some people then argue that wealth inequality is greater than income inequality so we should tax wealth. This is true, but also brings problems. Firstly, Scotland does not have the power to introduce a wealth tax. And then even if it did, much of this wealth is held in either pensions or property. People on higher professional salaries may appear to have substantial wealth but much of it is tied up in pension funds and cannot be released, and more is held in property which can only be released by selling the property. This means that many of those who appear to have many hundreds of thousands of pounds of 'wealth' will still be wholly reliant on income, and in turn, the capacity to tax that kind of wealth is much less than it may appear. Certainly, there are people who really do possess very substantial wealth and should make a much bigger contribution, and there are things that should be done to prevent the build-up of this wealth without tax being taken (for example, in myriad pension-related tax avoidance loopholes). But Scotland has no power to do anything about this, to fix the regressive element of National Insurance (rich people pay 10% less National Insurance after the first £42,000 of income, the rest being taxed at only 2%), to tackle corporation tax avoidance, or to introduce new taxes.

On top of this, a number of other ways that you might invest in the commons through tax and related policy are inaccessible for the Scottish parliament. For example, you could increase the minimum wage and then redirect the very substantial savings in tax credits that would result to other purposes (including subsidising the small number of small businesses which really would struggle to pay higher wages).

Put simply, we must be honest about the big limitations on what Scotland can do about tax, and how many things we ought to do that we simply can't. An alternative strategy is to understand the things we shouldn't need to do with tax. People often talk about tax being essential for redistributing wealth, but that in itself is a sign of failure. The need to redistribute wealth arises in the creation of substantially unequal wealth in the first place. It is because the economy creates so much in-work poverty alongside stratospheric wealth that the need to redistribute becomes so pressing. If you create a better economy with higher average pay and much less income inequality, the need to redistribute declines sharply. In fact, Britain is a very unequal country but actually has more progressive taxes than the much more equal Nordic countries. This is because the Nordic countries don't need to be as reliant on redistribution through progressive tax since their income distribution is much more progressive in the first place.

We should minimise the need to redistribute by creating an economy that does that for you (see chapter eight for strategies for creating a high-wage, more equal economy). If Scotland was to have the income distribution of an average Nordic country (no low pay, much less excessive wealth held by a few, a much more even spread of incomes, particularly in the middle) the impact would be startling. Without raising tax rates at all, achieving that more equal income distribution would automatically increase Scottish tax revenues by £4 billion simply by putting more money in more people's pockets. It would also save further billions of pounds in welfare costs—but that benefit would go to Westminster, not Scotland.

The only sustainable solution is to create a more equal economy, and no amount of tax credit or other form of subsidy for low pay will fix inequality (at best it will conceal it). But what can we do now? Scotland is facing cuts to its budget to something in the order of £1 billion. This will substantially harm our ability to invest in the commons and harm public services. It is suggested that we seek to raise approximately £500 million in additional tax measures to reduce the pressure from these cuts. In addition, this is a period in which poverty is on the rise and changes to benefits are going to make this worse. It is therefore suggested that another £200 million be raised to tackle the impacts of poverty. Ultimately, a total increase in tax revenues of approximately £700 million should be sought.

Aside from alleviating poverty and supporting public services, these tax proposals have two other important functions. Firstly, Scotland is a horrendously centralised country (see chapter seven for information on the urgent need to create a better local democracy in Scotland). At the moment local government raises less than 15 per cent of its income itself and so is reliant for nearly 90p in every pound it spends on grants from Holyrood. The local authorities that we have are undoubtedly in need of real reform and they must be democratised and made much more transparent and responsive to local need. But they also need the capacity to be responsible for their own actions, which would be enabled by substantial devolution of tax powers away from Holyrood and towards local government.

Finally, the Scottish Government has access to very few 'smart' tax levers which can be used for economic development purposes (smart meaning targeted and specific, not just general cuts in tax). For example, we cannot incentivise innovation, address VAT in low-margin sectors like tourism, or consider tax breaks in return for moving to the living wage (or tax rises to penalise those who don't). But there is one important incentive that can be created and that is to encourage the value of land to be rebalanced closer to its economic value—that is, the value that can be realised from the land based on economic activity taking place on it. Scotland has a major problem with the concentration of land ownership and this means getting access to land can be difficult.

But the deeper problem is that much of this land is held as a speculative asset (the value of large landholdings in Scotland has risen five times faster than the stock market in recent years). The incomes its owners make are not derived from the productive use of that land but in hoping that its speculative value will increase. This is harmful: land is an essential asset and if it is priced substantially above its economic value then it becomes very difficult to create a business case for land-based industries, so much of this land is kept empty, unproductive, and undeveloped. It also sharply pushes up the cost of housing, makes the development of towns and cities much more expensive, and is a general drag on the economy—all for private interests. This harmful cycle is encouraged by a tax system that does not seek to take any tax contribution from people based on their land ownership. A tax approach which incentivises the market to price land much closer to its economic value should therefore be put in place. Using a tax on large land wealth as a proxy for a wealth tax is also necessary.

With all of this information in mind, the following is a proposed package of tax measures. We raise the top rate (£150k and over) back to 50p, after being brought down to 45p under the last Tory-Lib Dem coalition government in 2013. A conservative estimate of an extra £20 million will be brought in from this. We should then introduce an additional tax band to seek a slightly bigger contribution from those on reasonably high salaries—perhaps those earning over £50,000. A higher tax rate for those in this band might be 43p in the pound, up from 40p. This would lead to a modest increase in the tax paid by affluent professionals and a more substantial tax rise for those on very high incomes. A cautious estimate would be that this would bring in approximately £180 million.

Over the course of a set period (perhaps five years), we should aim to substantially decentralise tax. Regional councils (as discussed in chapter seven) should aim to raise about 50 per cent of the money they spend at the end of this period. This decentralisation would offer opportunities for further changes, for example with Council Tax. There is a very strong economic case for keeping a tax on property to help to dampen the unsustainable rises in housing costs we've seen over recent decades. But this would be easier understood and fairer by basing the tax on the existing value of the house rather than the Council Tax method which involves bands of house prices based on values which are 25 years out of date. There is also a very strong case for an additional land value tax, as discussed above. However, it is unlikely that this scale of tax decentralisation could be achieved without contributing income taxes too. After all, income meets the three criteria of taxation set out above: it is a very good way of assessing what contribution an individual can afford to make, is very efficient, and is easy to understand.

The transition would work as follows. First, income tax at the national level would be cut, but a local income tax would be introduced at exactly the rate by which the national level was cut. People would pay precisely the same income tax but now a proportion of it would be distributed by regional councils. Each regional council's grant from central government would then be cut by exactly the same amount as the value of the tax being transferred so there would be no net change in budgets. Council Tax would then be replaced with a property value tax, again on a like for like basis so the total tax take is similar (although because a property tax is more progressive it would be spread more equitably). The existing taxes on non residential businesses would continue, other than when they are taken account of by the additional land value tax (discussed in more detail below). Aside from this additional tax, the decentralisation process in itself would not substantially change budgets or the balance between income and asset taxes.

Clearly there are some councils which are better able to raise tax due to the income profile of their population, just as is the case now. One of the reasons for retaining 50 per cent of the regional councils' funding from a block grant from Holyrood is to continue the use of equalisation methods which ensure that both ability to raise income and social need are taken into account in order that all regional councils have a level playing field.

In the past, central government has been excessively directive towards local government, but the whole point of decentralising tax is that central government should not dictate the exact tax strategies that a regional council should use. Central government should thus legislate for the powers to enable regional councils to raise these taxes and put in place the mechanisms for collecting them (where those mechanisms do not already exist). Once this is done it should be for a regional council to set the rates. There are many debates that can then be had about whether to move the balance of taxation away from income and towards taxing assets (which some argue would benefit the economy by discouraging non-productive 'rent-seeking' behaviour), whether asset taxes should be additional, or whether a different approach altogether should be taken. There is also circumstances in which a sales tax or hotel room tax could be appropriate. Crucially, this debate can take into account specific local conditions (for example where house prices are particularly high or where land ownership is particularly concentrated). Whatever decisions are made, it is for regional councils to answer to their electorate for their actions—and for central government to stop interfering.

However, part of this package should be used to reflect national policy priorities, for example in attenuating the effects of austerity. Both to act as a proxy wealth tax (since Scotland doesn't have the power to introduce one) and to incentivise the market to reprice land more accurately, land value tax should be introduced as part of the local tax measures. It should have a threshold based on unit value (i.e. only land worth more than a certain value per square metre would be taxed), with a mechanism for taxing very large landholdings of a lower value. This will mean that no residential tenants other than corporate renters will pay this tax as they already pay the property tax, and big commercial landowners (particularly corporations who are 'land banking') will pay more. While regional councils will have complete discretion over other taxes as outlined, there would be a minimum amount of Land Value Tax that each must raise. The aim would be to generate an additional £500 million from this tax in total. This compulsory minimum income would then be subtracted from the block grant, releasing £500 million to be used in national budgets to plug holes caused by austerity cuts. Authorities would be free to raise this tax further above the compulsory rate, giving them the flexibility to raise additional income.

Borrow to invest

Because of all the limitations outlined above, the remainder of the investment which we need to make in the commons will have to come from borrowing. In the past the term 'borrowing to invest' has been substantially misused and in many cases it simply meant borrowing to cover shortages in revenue (the recurring bills for wages, goods and services, and interest on borrowing that come from running public services and maintaining infrastructure), then redefining all revenue spending as an investment. Now in fact revenue spending is indeed an investment, but since this investment was already being made, borrowing to pay the recurring bills is borrowing to maintain the status quo, not borrowing to invest. Borrowing which is done to cover up the fact that you have been insufficiently honest about the cost of maintaining the commons (the public realm) because you want to avoid an uncomfortable conversation about tax is not a responsible way to manage budgets. Generally, you should aim to keep revenue spending (all recurring expenditure) broadly out of deficit by ensuring you have sufficient tax income to pay for them.

This is a fairly easy commitment to make in Scotland where borrowing powers are so limited and the parliament is so reliant on a block grant that it cannot run a deficit even if it wanted to and cannot build up debt because it doesn't have the powers. But this is a substantial problem because while you will want to pay for revenue from annual tax income, this is certainly not how you would generally want to pay for capital—capital meaning physical things that you only pay for once (although there may then be recurring costs for maintaining or operating them). Instead, capital is ideally paid for by borrowing to pay for it, not with recurring income.

Think about the difference between your weekly shopping and your mortgage. It would be very risky (and expensive) to pay for your weekly shopping using a bank loan. Eventually you'd have to pay it off and you'd have no remaining money—but you'd still have to pay for your shopping the next week. On the other hand it would be mad to buy a house using a credit card or by trying to do it from your wages. You're only going to buy one house at a time and probably stay in it for a long time. It just makes sense to borrow to pay for a house and to spread the cost over the whole period when you're living in that house. Hence we take out mortgages. On a national scale, this very generally means we should tax to pay for revenue and borrow to pay for capital. Unfortunately, Scotland does not have the proper range of powers to do this—though on the up side, we have no debt in Scotland and all our public debt is held by Westminster. Important to note here is that the analogy between a government and household budget is generally inaccurate because of the scale of complexity and investment—this is a me-firsters story, used to justify austerity with an argument that has no economic legitimacy.

To be able to invest in capital, we need two things: a reliable source of borrowing, and a mechanism for borrowing and investing. Not only the commons would benefit from better borrowing; the private sector in Scotland needs substantial investment of the right kind too (patient, supportive, focussed not on making the maximum profit from those who borrow but on helping achieve the maximum development possible). And with inflation at zero, the interest paid on government debt is at historically low levels.

One solution is to create a Scottish National Investment Bank (SNIB). This would have the purpose of lending to invest, not lending to speculate. It would invest to improve Scotland and it's economy, not to maximise shareholder profits. It would be run with full financial rigour but would be driven by a different ethos: providing long-term, patient funding for projects that meet social and environmental, as well as economic, criteria. It would lend to big national development projects, local authorities, and to large and developing Scottish businesses (smaller businesses would be more likely to borrow from local municipal banks which will be discussed below). It would aim to create real liquidity in Scotland, pumping money into the economy and stimulating transformation. It would of course need to select projects which will return the investment with sufficient interest to maintain the financial health of the bank, guaranteeing that borrowing will not be used to cover revenue.

As the Scottish Government is prohibited from substantial borrowing, the SNIB would need to be established as an independent company and possibly as a National Mutual Company (discussed further below). This just means that it would be a stand–alone 'business' which was not owned by government (and so was no risk to the wider public sector) but which was set up with rules so it worked for all of Scotland. It would not be intended to ever be solely owned by the government, but would rather bring together a wide range of public and voluntary financial institutions under its oversight, acting as a national coordinating body as well as a direct investor. It's role would be to ensure the best possible investment in Scotland and its future. Organisations such as housing associations, credit unions, local authorities and their municipal development banks (discussed below) would buy a stake in SNIB to help support its capitalisation.

The bank would need substantial capitalisation to make it transformational to Scotland's economy. Capitalisation simply means putting money into the bank which it can then lend. This is easier than it sounds because no banks actually have anything like the total money they lend out held in cash. A reasonable rule for SNIB would be that for every £10 it lends it should have £1 held in cash reserves. Treasury rules currently dictate that the Scottish Government can only borrow up to £304 million per year for capital (it also has an amount it can borrow to cover revenue in years of smaller tax returns). If the government put two-thirds of its Capital every year into the SNIB as its main lever for coordinating infrastructure investment, this would enable it to subscribe (promise and underwrite) £2 billion pounds for the bank to lend. In fact it would be hoped that only for the first two or three years would the Scottish Government actually put the £200 million into the bank, since by then the bank could secure sufficient amounts of its own revenue.

Once SNIB was capitalised to £2 billion, it would be able to invest £20 billion pounds in Scotland. It could also create long-term SNIB bonds to get further capitalisation from private and public investors (like local authority pension funds), which would see the SNIB as an attractive and safe option to put their money into. This is clearly a very substantial capitalisation indeed and would stimulate equally substantial economic activity as well as greatly improving the nation's infrastructure.

SNIB would also offer other benefits and services. It could create a common brand and marketing which would promote all local financial institutions (particularly the proposed municipal development banks) at a national level. It would offer technical assistance and capacity-building to create modern online banking services in local areas (including things like crowd-funding capacity and other new tech systems). It would put in place a set of common investment and economic development principles that become widely known and understood, and part of a national coordination structure backed by the Scottish Government, boosting its profile and credibility.

This package will encourage and incentivise the existing local financial institutions to professionalise and to have a municipal development bank in every local area. Support will be given nationally for the establishment of municipal banks where they don't exist, but the bulk of capitalisation of the municipal banks will come locally save for specific projects that require bigger investment money from SNIB.

The SNIB governance structure would be along similar lines to that of other investment bank models in Europe. At the top-level an overall board of governors would be made up of the various stakeholders, with an honorary position for the Scottish Government Finance Minister and Convener of the Scottish Parliament Finance Committee. A control committee, including representatives from the municipal development banks across Scotland, would ensure that the bank is carrying out its mandate, and then a third board works on a day to day level approving loans and making policy decisions.

A powerful SNIB would be a better route for the Scottish Government to invest in major project than relying on its own borrowing powers or revenue because the strict limits put on its capital spending by the Treasury mean that the total amount Scotland is allowed to spend would be gone in no time. The SNIB provides much larger scope for the sort of transformational investment plan that Scotland needs.

National Mutual Companies

However, the SNIB must be independent in its decisions on what loans to give, and therefore for big national investment projects that are absolutely essential to the public interest, the Scottish Government needs a new mechanism from which to borrow in large quantities, as it still could not afford to lend substantial sums directly from the SNIB. This means that we will need to create so-called 'special purpose vehicles' to make that investment. A special purpose vehicle is a company set up to carry out one specific task but designed so that the finances are self-contained and do not bring any risk to anyone else. Generally, they are some form of limited company which means that if the project they are set up to carry out goes wrong, they do not bring down a parent company (or in this case, the nation's public finances).

This can only be done in circumstances where a project can be financially self-sufficient, either because it is income-generating or because it provides paid-for services to government via long-term contracts. An example of the former would be a national housing company which could borrow to invest in housing and repay the investment through rental income; or a national energy company which does the same by building profit-making, energy generating infrastructure to repay loans. The latter might be a national childcare company which could invest heavily in creating really high-quality childcare facilities and employ more first-rate child carers with the Scottish Government paying it to provide this infrastructure and those services over an extended period.

But there have been very bad experiences with attempts to create structures which take government spending 'off the books', the most famous being the Private Finance Initiative. They have been incredibly inefficient and in many cases at least borderline corrupt. This is because they were largely created and run in secret by the financial industry for the financial industry (and this in the first half of the last decade, during which we now know the financial industry was totally out of control). They also lacked transparency and had little public interest represented in their governance (the structures through which they were run).

To remedy this, it is suggested that a new special purpose vehicle be developed: a 'national mutual company'. These would be private sector companies and so could borrow without limit. But they would be collectively owned and governed democratically. The best way to do this would be to constitute them so that every Scottish citizen would hold one non-tradeable share. This would give the people of Scotland collectively the legal ownership of the company and the democratic right to make decisions about that company. They would also be eligible for dividends from profits (a payment to all citizens from the profits of their national mutual companies). However, as company law is reserved to Westminster it is possible that this model would be blocked. If so, they should be set up with a constitution which behaved exactly as if all Scottish citizens were shareholders with a right for them to vote at the AGM and to still receive dividends.

These companies would then be limited only by their own business plan—as long as a business model is established that enables them to finance their activities, they would be unlimited in terms of how much investment they make. But they might also have an added bonus by genuinely engaging the wider population in major business decisions and in understanding and being interested in the governance of these large businesses. This could be a radical step in democratising the economy.

This has some problems, for example if the democratic aims of a national mutual company were at odds with the democratic aims of the Scottish Government, the Scottish Government could not command the national mutual. This would be a greater concern in areas where ideally a function should be fully under public control and it would be a cause for substantial concern if core functions like education or the health service were taken out of the direct control of government and put into national mutual companies. To avoid this, there should be national guidelines on what should remain a wholly-public function. There would be some debate on what constitutes a public function, but they would certainly include tax collection, the civil service, justice and policing, national defence, school education, the NHS, and transport infrastructure. In addition there would be a strong case for including energy, rail and bus travel, and possibly telephone and digital communication.

One area where particular consideration to inclusion on the wholly-public realm should be given is care. We have now had a National Health Service for 70 years, but the care sector remains fragmented, largely privatised, of very variable quality, and with clear evidence of poor value for money. Scotland should state a commitment to creating a National Care Service wholly in public ownership and should set a timetable for achieving it. The first step should be to create a national childcare service, completed by the end of the 2016 to 2021 parliamentary term.

If we do a simple international comparison we see just how inefficient the fragmented, for-profit childcare system we pay for is. Sweden spends 1.1 per cent of GDP on childcare (less than Scotland) and delivers universally excellent state-run nurseries from the end of parental leave to the start of school, with the average child:staff ratio being 5.3 children to every worker. This is the broad model that Scotland should follow. A mechanism for creating a national childcare service and making substantial investment in childcare facilities has been outlined above. There are many models for creating that infrastructure which can be explored. For example, given the likely long-term decline in retail provision on high streets, vacant retail units might be used to create bright, attractive childcare centres right in the heart of our towns.

Many providers in Scotland currently deliver excellent services, but we need to ensure that provision across the sector delivers a first-class learning and nurturing environment for all children and families. Perhaps we should think less in terms of 'care' and more in terms of 'participatory learning'. If you look at the policy approach taken in Sweden, or the Te Whariki statement in New Zealand, they respectively see a well-designed and socioculturally based national pre-school curriculum as the most important element in their pre-school system. Their approach is not just about feeding and watching children. It is based on research which indicates that the brain sensitivity to language, numeracy, social skills, and emotional control all peak before the age of four and that the best way to support children's development is by enabling creative learning relationships. Early years education is seen as vital, as is continuity between early years and primary school education.

The presence of an early years 'curriculum' does not mean that early years learning should become overly formalised. Rather early years education should be a relaxed, nurturing, and respectful environment based on play and opportunities to enjoy the outdoors. Indeed, many providers currently promote a child-led approach utilising local outdoor environments as a source of learning. Indoors, the learning environment should be 'home-like' with the emphasis being fun and happiness—a 'compliment to the home'. Crucially there is no formal assessment or evaluation of the individual child (though there is evaluation of the processes and dialogues used). The emphasis is on relationships, social skills, and the needs of the individual. It is predicated on a mission of 'what would you like to do?', not on 'how to do it', with children and teachers encouraged to come up with their own methods through participation and collaboration. In New Zealand, the emphasis is on the learning partnership between teachers, parents, child, and cultural context. In Sweden they spend half the day outside (even in the winter), exercise is very important, and before the age of seven literacy and writing skills aren't pushed—yet these children end up with the best literacy skills in Europe. Food is healthy and fresh, and staff are treated as professionals. We can have a childcare service like this in Scotland.

We know how important early years development is for the long-term wellbeing of a child, and so we should design our childcare system as a priority to focus on positive development. As well as high-quality facilities, this will mean highly skilled and supported staff. Professionalising childcare has two important impacts. First, we improve child development and wellbeing, and second, we invest in a sector which is dominated by low-pay work predominately carried out by women. The low pay among the largely female workforce in the care sector contributes to the gap in pay between men and women in Scotland. If we can take a sector which should be professionalised anyway and create more high-pay jobs for women (and particularly young women), then we tackle the pay gap. This is one example of how making investment via the commons can design much more effective systems with multiple benefits than can be achieved by following the doctrine of 'let them do as they please'.

Improving the Public Sector

There are challenges which will be faced by Scotland's public services over coming years. Westminster's aggressive austerity policies will increase poverty and therefore increase demand on public services. And this will happen at the same time as £1 billion is cut from the funding of public services because of the same Westminster austerity obsession. Above it has been suggested how Scotland could raise up to an additional £500 million to lessen the impact of these cuts. But this is only one method, and we need other responses now.

Public sector 'reform' has become a pet subject of me-first politics, mainly as a cover for cutting public services. However, this does not mean that all-of-us-first politics should dodge the question of the shape and nature of effective organisations, nor that it shouldn't question the way public services are currently structured, organised, and delivered. It's just that the aim at the outset should be to create better public services and not to cut provision or costs. Getting more value from investment should simply be an outcome of getting organisations right.

In this it is worth being clear about the difference between 'management approaches' (which have been much of the focus of organisational development over the me-first years, so convinced were they that it is managers who make organisations run) and genuine organisational development. In recent years there has been a wide range of new thinking on what organisations are and how they should be structured. In almost all cases there is a focus on flattening hierarchies (or in some cases abolishing them altogether), on greater peer-management (the people delivering services managing them too), and on focusing on values rather than targets. Some approaches focus on what might be called 'circularity': that power and knowledge will sometimes flow down whatever hierarchies exist but that power and knowledge should equally flow upwards from the frontline.

In all of this there is an explicit rejection of me-first models which treat organisations as if they are 'machines' or 'markets'—and often seem to view staff as a kind of flaw in the system which might mess up the operation of that machine or market if they're not closely managed. A much better approach is to trust staff and base organisations on a belief in the best in people. It people drive an organisation through their commitment, morals, and values, it has a much better chance of becoming an organisation of people for people. The evidence is that this makes them not only 'emotionally better' but also much, much more productive too.

All of these approaches are critical of the box-ticking, performance indicator-driven approaches to organisational management. Some are equally critical of rigid, long-term plans. There is some really fascinating case study work now available on self-managing organisations which continually respond and adapt to their environment because they are driven not by indicators or strategies but by strong guiding values which all employees support. In these organisations you get constantly evolving strategies based on the changing circumstances around them. There is a consistent emphasis on better design of service and organisation through fully involving both those delivering and those receiving services from the very beginning and continuously. There is also a constant emphasis on learning, with both individuals and the organisation as a whole continuously learning from each other, from user feedback, and from past practice. In all of this, moves towards flatter structures also mean flatter income spreads within organisations. Since this is a goal for the wider economy, the public sector should be leading in reducing its own income inequality.

Many of these approaches are now routinely used in more

innovative businesses. Some are based on genuinely radical shifts
such as manager-less organisations (where self-organising units using
modern technology manage themselves), new decision-making models
of neither command-and-control nor consensus, and approaches to
expectation about how people should 'be' in their work (challenging
the ingrained assumption that 'professionalism' involves rejecting
emotional engagement with what you do). A proposal for a new series
of National Policy Academies is discussed below, one of which should
be established as a centre for radical and far-reaching thinking about the
way organisations and institutions should operate. It would be a centre of
excellence in service design, flatter organisational development, and new
approaches to self-management within organisations.

Digital Currency

One final way that Scotland would ideally be able to invest in the
commons would be to use targeted quantitative easing (the effective
'printing of money' which in recent years has been used to hand many
hundreds of millions of pounds to the big banks). Unfortunately
Scotland has absolutely no powers in this area. However, it would be
possible to create a parallel Scottish digital currency and do something
similar with it.

This currency would be digital and act as a complement to the
national currency, limited in its design to Scotland, pegged to sterling
and with a payment system—ScotPay—without transaction costs.
You would spend it using your mobile phone or another device, and it
could be used to pay for tax bills or other public services. A six month
campaign before launch would get a large number of retailers and small
businesses also accepting it, who would be incentivised to use it for their
own costs due to the free transaction mechanism, as well as paying for
taxes like non-domestic rates with it. It would then be recycled into
the economy by using it to fund modest pay rises in the public sector.
Gradually it is hoped that the circulation of the currency through
businesses, the public sector, and consumers would make it a vibrant
stimulus to local services and businesses.

If Scotland created £1 billion pounds worth of digital currency that would mean that every citizen could be given £250 worth to spend—a national stimulus package which has been proven to help kick-start economic activity, particularly in local economies and among the poorest sections of society who tend to spend what they have rather than save.

The ScotPound central bank would carefully monitor the impact of ScotPound over the course of the first year, before making a decision of how (if at all) to put more ScotPounds into circulation (it would not be helpful if people became excessively over-reliant on the currency as a total of their income). In the second year, ScotPound stimulus could be approached in a more targeted way to the poorest sections of society, or it could be democratised by giving a set amount to communities to decide how to use it via participatory budgeting. Either way, this would inject a billion pounds into the Scottish economy and increase demand, without any increase in personal debt.

National Policy Academies

But the commons isn't just about money and services; it's about ideas and policy too. At the moment Scotland is not enormously well served with the infrastructure for creating new public policy thinking. It has few think tanks and they're poorly funded. Academia has not engaged in creating new ideas for public policy to anything like the degree it might want to. Scotland's political parties do not have particularly strong policy capacity and other institutions like trade unions have often focussed on producing critiques of existing policy. This has left the civil service as the institution which is tasked with doing much of Scotland's original thinking. For a country with so much thinking capacity in its institutions it is disappointing that we don't have a richer debate about policy.

It is therefore proposed that Scotland should create a series of National Policy Academies. Each would cover a major area of public policy (such as 'housing, town planning and transport' or 'policing, criminal justice and community safety'). Some might cover more operationally-focussed thinking (the centre for excellence in service and organisation design suggested above, a centre for good practice in participatory democracy discussed in chapter seven). Each would be attached to a university, and the civil service would second a significant proportion of its staff to these Academies, working closely with academics and people from civil society (organisations might second some of their staff for specific projects). Importantly, these would be open, public institutions. The purpose would be to take the thinking about public policy out of the 'black box' where people only get to see consultations and final decisions. Academies would be democratically governed and all of the work would be free for everyone to see and to engage with. Interested members of the public would find easy routes for taking ideas to the Academies, working with a variety of people to develop potentially radical proposals.

In turn, the civil service would no longer undertake blue-sky thinking and would focus on being an implementation agency. Government (and others involved with public policy such as political parties) would then source blue-sky thinking from Academies by posing them problems or questions and asking for solutions and answers. Academies need not give back a single, unified and universally agreed answer, but might send back a range of options or a broad solution with a range of different approaches. Certainly, disagreement or doubt about precisely the best way to do things would not be seen as a weakness in an Academy.

Then of course it would be for the democratically elected government to decide which view to implement, whether to agree with the idea at all, whether to send the idea back for further work, or whether to do something else altogether. Whatever the outcome, the process of doing this thinking collectively and in public would greatly enrich Scotland's democracy and its 'collective intellect'.

This does not mean that everything is ideal in the implementation phase of public policy in Scotland. While the Scottish Government's internal legal advice does a good job of keeping the Scottish Government out of court and in line with the law, it is almost universally seen as being excessively risk averse. Very often good policy ideas are blocked by legal advice that they would potentially contravene European law. But 'potentially' and 'definitely' are quite different, as are 'may face a legal challenge' and 'would be likely to lose a legal challenge'. After all, virtually everything could in theory face a legal challenge. It is of particular concern that practices which appear to be normal in other

European countries are deemed illegal in Scotland.

This is not how big corporations behave. When a corporation's lawyers tell them something can't be done, in the well-known phrase the corporation will demand 'better lawyers'. It is this asymmetry—government lawyers who seek to avoid a fight against corporate lawyers determined to win the fight—which has blocked so much progressive policy.

Again, the government lawyers do a good job of providing advice, but the public deserve to have an approach to the law which is every bit as determined to win as the private sector's approach. The Scottish Government should therefore set up a 'legal hit squad'. Where the routine advice by the legal service is that something can't be done (and where the government sees it as a sufficient priority), the government should be able to call on a specialist team of lawyers whose sole purpose is to make sure the government wins, to find work-arounds, to take a more aggressive approach to risk assessment, and so on. This 'hit squad' might be attached to a legal National Policy Academy.

Indicate to educate

In all of this we should have an ability to judge how good the overall performance of the commons is. At the moment we have many indicators of progress, but there are so many it's difficult for most citizens to keep track. Thusly, there are a very small number of key indicators which have a prominence way above any others—and one above all. That this indicator—GDP—tends to reinforce the interests of corporations may not come as much of a surprise. By chasing 'economic growth' as measured by GDP, we have pursued stupid policies designed to improve profits in the very short term. Almost all other indicators (apart perhaps from inflation and unemployment) come a distant second.

The trick is to get a balance: too few indicators and it is impossible to make a balanced assessment of what is happening in society; too many and it is very difficult for people to understand what the indicators may be showing. What Scotland needs is a limited 'dashboard' of indicators—perhaps a maximum of ten—which give a more balanced picture. They should be issued together and no one of them should be given presentational priority when they are issued. There can be debate about what should be covered and what indicator gives the best measure, but as well as GDP, inflation, and unemployment there should be something on economic equality, wages and living standards, health and wellbeing, and carbon emissions (there are many others people might suggest such as innovation and productivity and there will be debate about the best measure of each). People should become familiar with the dashboard and should be helped to interpret what they mean for progress in our society.

In the period between the Scottish elections in 2016 and the next set (probably in 2021), Scotland's commons will come under attack from a hostile austerity agenda being set in London. But far from cowering in response, the set of measures proposed above would be an ambitious and powerful rebuilding of the commons in Scotland.

Chapter Seven
Nothing about us without us is for us

In the previous chapter we explored how to build a really powerful commons in Scotland and how it can invest in and design policy and services to really improve people's lives. But if it is truly to be the commons, then it must not just be 'for us' but 'by us'. The age when a social, economic and political elite ran society in secret 'for our own good' is over. But a new age of truly participatory democracy has not yet been fully born. We still have little say beyond a vote every four or five years and we often have insufficient rights even to know what is being done 'for our own good' with a host of excuses such as 'national security', 'commercial confidentiality' and 'protecting diplomatic relations' being used to ensure that much of government is still done in secret. But perhaps most unpalatable of all is the attitude still prevalent among many administrators (and not a few politicians) that frankly 'the people' aren't fit or capable of making complex decisions for themselves and so must be managed. By administrators.

Not only is this no longer acceptable as a philosophy for our mutual government, again and again it has been shown to fail and fail spectacularly. The problem with elite rule is that too often elites simply agree with each other. When elite groups of experts meet in private to make decisions they see weapons of mass destruction in Iraq but fail to notice there was any risk in the uncontrolled deregulation of the financial industries. They then conclude that the fall-out from Iraq must be met with more bombing and that the massive financial crash must be met with equally massive handouts of public money to the people responsible for the crash. Elite decision-making doesn't work because good decisions are not made by groups which all come in with one mindset and make the decisions in an environment where they can't be challenged. Participatory democracy is not only morally right, it is a more effective means of making decisions.

Creating a participatory democracy in Scotland means following one simple motto: nothing about us without us is for us. If decisions or actions impact on us but we have no role in shaping or influencing these decisions or actions, then they cannot be 'ours', of us, or of the commons. Thankfully, years of exciting new practices in democracy means that all the tools needed to make Scotland a nation of its people, by its people, and for its people is something we can achieve now.

A true local democracy

The first and most pressing problem is the massive democratic deficit that Scotland faces below the level of Holyrood. It is important that we understand that absolutely nowhere in Europe and probably nowhere in the developed world is as centralised and centrally-controlled as Scotland. If you look at indicators of just how bad Scotland is at making decisions nowhere near the people they affect, you cannot help but feel shocked.

Scotland's councils have 30 times the population size of an average European country's local councils, which means that the average European citizen's voice is 30 times louder in local decisions than the average Scottish citizen. The land area of a Scottish 'local' authority is 50 times bigger than the land size of the average European local authority. So we can assume that on average, a Scottish citizen will have to travel 50 times as far to get to their council headquarters. Scotland is the only European country that only has one layer of local government. The ratio of elected councillors to citizens in Scotland is six times worse than the European average, which means that the average European councillor can be six times more responsive than can a Scottish councillor.

Almost everyone who has been in government over the last 20 years shares responsibility for this—no political party has a respectable track record when it comes to creating Europe's most centralised country. Scotland should be ashamed of this track record—and politicians who make arguments in favour of being the least democratic country among their peers should also be ashamed. People are right to be very suspicious of politicians who say they are 'empowering' them without actually giving them any new power.

There is only one true form of power that communities and citizens can hold in a democracy and that is the power to make decisions about policy and resources through democratic means. Put bluntly, if you can't 'fire' the people who make a bad decision for your town, you're not empowered. Scotland's vast local authorities mean that it is almost impossible to hold them to account for individual decisions.

There is only one solution: Scotland must move into the mainstream of local democracy in Europe and recognise that some decisions are national and some decisions are regional—but some decisions really are local. We need genuinely local councils—because the ones that we have are regional. Scotland needs a new layer of community democracy so communities (and not sprawling regions) can make their own decisions.

This does not involve expensive reorganisation of local government. The officer staff in existing authorities already work to direction from different committees within the existing councils. All that is required is that they take direction on different functions from two different councils. The existing councils should be properly described as what they in effect are: regional councils. In this context there is a case for exploring some mergers, particularly of the smaller councils but also in places where recognised regional areas are currently divided (such as Lanarkshire and Ayrshire).

Below this level would be a layer of genuinely local councils. The process of identifying where these are and what size they are should be driven by the communities involved. We should be very comfortable with wide differences in size between these local councils. Some might consist of a small group of adjacent rural villages. Some might be the size of a small town, some the size of a big town. Cities might be considered single authorities—or areas within cities (for example Govan in Glasgow) might wish their own local representation. The important thing is that however these councils are structured, the communities they serve must feel that they are genuinely 'their' councils.

At this community democracy level, local councillors should not be paid (other than expenses) and council meetings should take place in the evening so all citizens have an opportunity to become community politicians. These councils should be adaptable and innovative in achieving a diverse and representative council; for example holding alternative meeting hours to make participation possible for more women, considering a system of discretionary assistance for low-pay workers, or ensuring that materials, buildings, and services are accessible for disabled Scots. The cost of running these local councils will be minimal, however, they should have the right to be powerful. Scotland should aspire to devolve real power as far as possible, whenever possible.

A mechanism for doing this might be to establish a set of 'reserved' powers at each level of government. For example, it is absolutely essential that even where delivery of health or education has local flexibility it must remain the duty of national government to ensure (and in the event of problems, enforce) consistent national quality standards. Law, justice and the policing of major crimes will remain at national level, as will national transport infrastructure, taxation and budgeting, national economic development and so on. The regional councils would need to retain responsibility for social work, waste collection, regional planning decisions, and much of local transport, as well as the powerful new roles proposed in this book such as running development banks and energy companies. After this it would be the right of each layer of government to 'draw down' powers as they develop and feel comfortable taking more responsibility. This process of allowing powers to move closest to where they are going to impact is known as subsidiarity.

There must also be serious consideration given to the way regional councils (the current local authorities) operate. Until the 1990s these councils were comparatively open and transparent and largely operated on a committee structure. This committee system made most of the decisions and were open to the public and to the media. But throughout the 1990s, councils were driven towards a form of 'cabinet government' where a small executive working with unelected officials carried out most of the decision-making in private with little or no transparency. This was followed by the proliferation of 'arms length executive organisations' (ALEOs): semi-private companies which run public services but outside the democratic system. Council executives can then appoint their own boards (often paid, usually appointing their own councillors to these paid posts on top of their council salaries) and the whole process can be run almost completely outside of real democratic oversight. This means of working in local authorities is fundamentally wrong. It has led to many citizens concluding that 'it doesn't make any difference—the council will do what it wants anyway and no-one can stop them'. Very often, the citizens are right.

Regional government must return to an open, democratic committee system for decision-making. ALEOs must not be permitted in any area which can be considered core council business, and a process of being able to challenge the set up of ALEOs should be available. Councils must meet regularly and in public. Major decisions should not be arrived at outside of the public committee and council structure.

One of the biggest problems in local authorities is lack of proper scrutiny. Scotland's local newspapers have struggled along with most of the print media. Few can cover local government in the detail they once could, and many local papers would not survive without advertising income from the local authority, meaning they are less likely to criticise council activities.

There are a few possible responses to this. One is to support local journalism through financial support from central government. Another would be to support local citizen journalism. Another would be the (compulsory if need be) use of the techniques of participatory democracy discussed below. At the very least, the low level of trust in local authorities is such that serious consideration should be given to setting up 'citizen forums'. In effect, these would be a committee of citizens which would meet to monitor decisions made by the council to ensure good practice is used and that the views of citizens are being properly sought and subsequently not ignored.

Creating participatory democracy

All of this would be nothing more than remedial, bringing Scottish democracy up to the basic standards of its European neighbours. Scotland should then push forward and create genuinely innovative systems of participatory democracy. It should start by creating a National Policy Academy dedicated to democratic reform (a Democracy Academy) but which is also resourced to be a facilitating body. It should employ staff able to run mini-publics, participatory budgeting, public deliberation, policy conferences, and so on. It should have an advisory role on effective public communication, good practice in consultation, and good democratic practice generally.

Government should then use radical new practices in how it seeks opinion and advice. Firstly, it must change how it seeks the views of stakeholders and citizens. Consultation is an essential part of the work of government but for many of those consulted, it is now seen through cynical eyes. This is largely due to bad practice: consultation is often brought in to the decision-making process far too late after key decisions have been made, leaving people feeling that they are not being consulted but being asked to offer opinions on fairly minor aspects of implementation. This feeling of 'coercive consultation' is disempowering, further exacerbated when people see little connection between what people have put in their consultation responses and what then emerges as the final decision—the so-called 'black box' problem where you can see what goes in and what comes out but have no idea what happened in between.

This happens in part because of the usual pressures of workload and in part because people tend to do things 'as they've always been done'. But there is certainly a part of this which really is driven by a desire to use consultation not to seek views but to manage stakeholders into accepting decisions which have already been made. Unsurprisingly this is known as DAD (Decide, Announce, Defend)—an undemocratic practice.

Where possible, consultations should be replaced by co-production and collaboration with the users of services. Whichever approach is taken, it should begin at the earliest possible point in policy development, to help frame the question and the solution, and not just to shape implementation. If there is a network of National Policy Academies (as discussed in chapter 6) then by nature they should be doing the early thinking anyway, hopefully outside the context of 'big p' politics and in an open and democratic way. Individual Policy Academies should work with the Democracy Academy to produce the best and most open consultation process possible, then use the best and most open process for identifying what has come out of consultation, adapting to change thinking if the results contradict what people expect. Of course, because Policy Academies are open and participative, there should be continuous opportunities for citizens to follow, engage with, and propose changes to the development of thinking. Government and the civil service will of course have to consult on the implementation phase of policies too and they should also work with the Democracy

Academy to follow best practice at all stages. This will form a robust and comprehensive system of public deliberation over policy development that goes beyond simple consultation.

We should then look closely at how government receives advice. At the moment the usual practice is to set up an 'expert group' to consider the issue and give advice. This immediately has the problem of 'everyone coming into the room thinking the same thing'. It also has serious problems with representation ('experts' are virtually never in low pay, marginalised, or vulnerable groups) and continually raises the problem of vested interests (the financial sector has been enormously over-represented on expert groups over recent decades—and we all paid the price). But there are problems even in the case of more balanced 'stakeholder groups' where not everyone thinks the same. Primarily, these can become inherently risk averse, reaching a lowest common denominator between vested interests, and they generally tend to result in the status quo rather than change.

There is a better way to do this, and in Scotland we already use it every day of the week all over the country. It is known as a 'mini-public' (literally a group of people selected to represent a smaller cross section of the population as a whole) and most people will know them as juries in the court system. Here ordinary members of the public represent our collective interests by listening to evidence from experts, drawing conclusions, and making decisions from what they have heard. The same process can be used for almost any decision-making process. If you want to think about why we should extend the use of mini-publics to public policy decision-making, think about it the other way round. How would you react if jury trials were removed and instead guilt or innocence were decided by a group of people appointed by government who were all wealthy and who made their decision completely in secret. It wouldn't be acceptable—and it shouldn't be in public policy.

Every time government needs to seek advice it should set up a mini-public to provide that advice. These must represent society—women, minorities, and those in low pay are groups that are particularly likely to have their voice excluded from or marginalised in decision-making and so particular care should be taken to ensure that they are represented in mini-publics. There are a number of forms—citizens' juries, planning cells, consensus conferences, deliberative polls, and citizens' assemblies. It is important to be clear that the use of mini-publics should not imply that expert opinion is not essential or that it should not be what drives the final decision, it's just that the expertise and the decision should be separated. A mini-public should be given the question on which advice is sought and presented with a range of expert views in evidence sessions (and presented with consultation responses where available). They should then be free to cross-examine witnesses, ask for additional information, request other witnesses, and so on. They should then come to a conclusion and present it to government. Of course, as with Policy Academies, government is the democratically elected body and must always be free to reject advice, but they should by law provide written explanation available in the public domain for why they decided to reject the advice of a mini-public if they decide to do so.

There will be some occasions where it is not appropriate to use a mini-public. For example, in the event of a sudden public health emergency or in extremely detailed legal matters. However, exemptions will mean that there is a tendency once again to 'do what we always did' and get in the same group of experts. The government should therefore be required to use a mini-public whenever advice is sought and while there would be a right to an exemption, the government should be required to produce a written explanation of why an exemption was enacted. 'The people are too stupid to understand this' should never be a reason.

Another practice which should be 'triggered' at specific moments is participatory budgeting. Increasingly widely used by citizens across Scotland (although not 'mainstreamed' into government institutions), participatory budgeting involves citizens and affected groups being involved in the process of creating budgetary priorities. The process is deliberative—people don't just 'vote' for what they want money spent on but think together about the consequence of what money therefore wouldn't be spent on. Participatory budgeting not only improves the quality of the budgeting process, it also helps communities to learn about and understand the complexity of managing competing priorities when allocating resource. Just as with mini-publics, public sector organisations should be required to use some form of participatory budgeting whenever they are required to set budgets, or should produce a written statement of why this has not been done.

These are all existing practices which have been extensively developed over time and will make an enormous difference to how government operates and how open it is. However they are all still 'producer-led' (because they can only be used when government says they can and citizens don't have a right to make them happen themselves). So Scotland should go further and create a system for influencing and shaping the nation which is in the control of citizens. The name 'ting' has been increasingly used to describe this idea.

Ting is an old Norse word for a kind of informal council of citizens or their representatives. It involved people gathering at a specific place to discuss and make collective decisions about whatever they wanted to discuss. Tings were common in Scotland a millennium ago and there are still places whose name is derived from 'ting' (such as Dingwall). Reinventing Tings could prove to be a remarkable democratic innovation in Scotland.

A 21st century ting would be a gathering of people to consider a subject, not just to discuss it but to come up with ideas and solutions and test them. For this to happen it must be linked to a source of power, at either national or local level, and must be informed by the understanding of whatever issue is under discussion. It would be a place (which could be anything from an existing town hall, to a dedicated venue, to a converted bus, or even an online space) where people could get together and discuss specific issues. Eventually everyone in Scotland would be close to a local Ting; the first stop for public service providers to collaborate with citizens in re-imaging and designing public services. They would evolve as we all re-learn citizenship; people would decide how they wanted to use them and adapt as necessary. Ideas can come from anywhere: citizens, community groups (or a club, association, or group of local businesses), or public service to propose a project. This would then be advertised at the Ting and people would be invited to come together to discuss it. The Ting could then produce as many ideas or thoughts on this as those who participate come up with. It might seek to come to a single consensus solution, or be happy testing a number of less well-developed ideas—what is crucial is that it is citizen-led and adapts thusly.

There are be two structurally important aspects of Tings. First, there would need to be a means of feeding these ideas into government in an effective and meaningful way—these are not just talking shops but ideas factories. Sharing the learning from Tings will be important: when there are sufficient Tings in the network, dealing with a wide range of issues at all levels, the accumulated learning will help inform politicians about the issues that matter. The one immediate route would be for Tings to be networked with the National Policy Academies—if a Ting comes up with a great idea for boosting tourism nationally, there would be a place to take that idea for further development. Another route would be for Tings to invite politicians and civil servants (or local government officers since many ideas may be locally focussed) to come and hear a presentation of the ideas involved. There are myriad possibilities for feeding ideas into government and other decision-making bodies.

The second important aspect of Tings is that they need to be well networked with each other. Tings should be able to adopt projects being run by other Tings, take their ideas, and develop them further, or in different directions. It should be a network of places which build up the capacity of citizens to shape their own society for us all (including children and young people) and to learn to be active citizens. But these must also be seen as incredibly valuable resources, harnessing the creativity and ideas of citizens to help build a better Scotland.

Tings must be open, neutral places not dominated by partisan politics—but designed to prevent 'neutral' meaning a recreation of traditional power structures which overwhelmingly suit the opinions of white, non-disabled, straight men. They must also be trusted spaces where people not only feel able to participate without feeling threatened but feel that there is genuine equality in access to them, and that the work they do is properly valued. They will need facilitation and support as they grow and define themselves. The development of Tings should become a primary responsibility of the proposed Democracy Academy.

One possible route for the ideas emerging from Tings to take would be a 'national policy conference' or national Ting. These are big, discursive national conferences which engage substantial proportions of the population in the process (in Iceland they had one in every 200 citizens involved and in Brazil they have involved five million people over the last ten years). National policy conferences are the end result of a year-long process of identifying issues people want to discuss and developing the questions and ideas to be considered. This could all be done through the network of Tings. The final Ting or conference is a chance for lots of people to engage in a big, high-profile, national discussion about an issue not set by government but chosen by citizens— and to influence national politics.

By developing these ideas into robust and lasting structures, the government can cease to use private sector consultancy firms and in particular the large, generalist ones which have become the default source of advice for many parts of government. Large accountancy and legal firms have pitched themselves as 'honest brokers' whom government can come to for a 'neutral' assessment of what is in the public interest. This practice is little understood by the public but is of very serious concern. These companies not only shape public policy through these contracts to provide advice to government, they then advise their commercial customers how to navigate and benefit from public policy. There is a clear conflict of interests here; perhaps the most blatant recent example was the company that advised the Westminster government on the price of the privatisation of the Royal Mail, at the same time as advising its investment clients to buy the shares because they were undervalued. There are many examples of so-called independent advice changing public policy in a way that financially benefits the company providing that advice (for example they often propose mergers and then win contracts to oversee the process of the merger). There is absolutely no need for this and with the processes proposed above, the practice of using private sector consultancy to shape public policy should be ended.

Democratising the unelected public realm

However, government is not the only part of the public realm which should belong to us. There are many organisations and institutions which are part of the commons but not directly part of government (quangos, agencies, universities and colleges, and so on). At the moment the way that these institutions are managed and governed is at best short of democratic best practice, and at worst entirely undemocratic. In the case of agencies and quangos, generally the governing body is appointed by a government Minister and generally (other than sometimes in the case of the chair of a governing body) it is a mainly private and secret process. Civil servants make suggestions and the Minister chooses between them. With some other organisations such as universities, there is absolutely no democratic element at all. The governing body appoints itself in perpetuity based on recommendations coming from the chief executive's office (even though the chief executive is who the Board is supposed to govern).

All of this results in a situation where large parts of the governance of the public realm (and the governance of lots of key public functions and the oversight of large amounts of public money) is done by a self-selecting group which has absolutely no requirement to respond to anything or anyone other than themselves. And of course, the profile of these people is heavily skewed towards the very wealthy and involves a very disproportionate number of people from within the same social networks.

This has all the problems of 'expert groups', except these people are often not selected for their expertise but because they are 'respected' (as in 'the respected business leader...' or 'the respected lawyer...'). Of course, being respected is a subjective idea and in this case almost always means 'respected by other business leaders and other lawyers'. And being respected may well mean not challenging orthodoxies or asking difficult questions. This is government by one social class, appointed by that same social class, and answerable only to that social class.

This semi-feudal model really should be challenged. It offers no space for debate or consideration of the role, function, or actions of an institution on the part of its stakeholders or those it affects. Students or staff have little to no say on the strategy or policy of a university, artists no say on the policy of its funding agency, the registered disabled no say on who might be appointed as a 'disability tsar', and so on. If there were democratic elections to the governing bodies of these institutions, not only would the boards be much more reflective of the views of a wider group in society and bring in new blood and fresh talent from groups which currently appear excluded (for example, anyone on low or medium incomes), it would also require an honest and open debate about the role and purpose of the institution and its strategy. In almost every case, it is possible to identify a coherent 'community' which these institutions serve. There is simply no reason they cannot open up democratic elections to these governing bodies, requiring people to stand on manifestos explaining what they would do if they were part of that governing body. Improved digital technology is now readily available to make such elections eminently doable.

One crucial part of democracy is lobbying: the right of interest groups to seek to influence politics. It is right that lobbying and the presentation of ideas and arguments to politicians from outside politics is seen as fundamental to democracy. However, there are two problems with the current lobbying system. The first is that 'disorganised opinion' (which is to say groups of people who do not have organisations which represent their interests) are greatly disadvantaged, and this group of people are more likely to be the more marginalised and vulnerable in society. The aforementioned proposals in this chapter will go a long way to addressing that problem. The second problem is the complete asymmetry of influence and access involved. It is all very well to say that lobbying is good for democracy but that cannot ignore the fact that some lobby groups have enormous resources and privileged access. Certainly a community which faces an opencast mine can make representation to government—but big mining companies can pay for extensive direct access, take politicians on all-expenses-paid 'fact-finding' trips, hire PR companies to place lots of sympathetic media stories, commission expensive economic research to 'prove' their case, and so on. The fight between these interests is deeply unfair.

There is no easy or immediate solution to this; people are free to spend their money how they see fit, newspapers are free to write whatever stories they want, and so on. However, there is one thing we can do, and that is to make sure that everyone knows when a fight is unfair. This is simple: every lobbying campaign has a budget, whether it is an internal allocation of money for the purpose or a contract with an external lobbyist. Along with the registration for lobbyists, every lobby campaign should simply disclose its existence and its budget. No-one's rights or freedoms have been impinged, but the public (and politicians) will be in a position to make their own judgement about whether expensively obtained PR is the same thing as fair representation.

The best safeguard against undue lobbying and a host of other abuses of democracy is Freedom of Information. If 'the state' is simply part of the commons and if we own those commons collectively, the concept of information being withheld from us on a routine basis is very problematic. The Freedom of Information legislation in Scotland has made an enormous difference—but is still too restricted and often comes under attack from those who do not wish to share information. The legislation should be strengthened to remove as many exemptions as possible—and in particular the commercial confidentiality exemptions which allow private companies to operate public services without having the duty to provide clear and transparent information about how it operates. FoI should be extended to all government contractors and the ability of the Information Commissioner to hold authorities to account should be both strengthened and speeded up.

One issue which is worth considering but which is fraught with difficulties is the right of recall. This just means that where politicians have not lived up to what they promised their electorate, or are involved in activity which their electorate believes questions their fitness to represent them, then the electorate has a right to 'recall' that politician and force a new election. The difficulties exist since sometimes politicians really do have to make difficult decisions and political opponents can use recall in negative ways. It can also make politicians even more risk-averse—but this issue and solutions should be explored in the Democracy Academy.

Another essential element of democracy is a media willing to hold government to account. Britain's media is very unbalanced, owned as it is by a tiny number of individuals and corporations. Scotland's media is also unbalanced (with almost complete opposition to independence for example), but equally worrying is that it is greatly underfunded. In most cases an entire parliament is supposed to be held to account by one or at most two journalists from each newspaper. This is insufficient and for reasons both of balance and capacity, action should be taken.

The economics of news publishing is changing rapidly as readership is dropping off with more and more people getting their news online and more and more print newspapers picking up stories from online coverage. But a sustainable business model for Scotland-scale online news and proper journalism is not easy to do 'in your spare time'. It is therefore suggested that government help fund journalism, focussing on online and citizen journalism. It is important that this is done in a fair and even-handed way: encouraging more online news sites to monitor public life in Scotland will enhance democracy, especially if that strategy addresses the obscene inequalities in media representation and journalism by supporting the engagement of those less likely to create content such as women and ethnic minorities.

We need system-wide change if we truly want to innovate with democracy in our education system. We need a sustainable collaboration between politicians, civil servants, the educational establishment, the institutionalised profession, local authorities, pupils, and parents. Tings could connect decision-makers and service users regularly, allowing them to come together to assess development, implementation, and strategies for education, at both a local and national level. As a vital part in developing the concept of citizenship, education should not be limited to the bullet points in a subject syllabus. A focus on projects and problem solving as well a comprehensive education on local politics will help learners to be resourceful, enterprising, and empowered. This also involves a holistic approach to their interaction in the school: whether in helping develop budgets for classroom equipment, cooking food for school lunches, or aiding janitorial staff in building management. Real democracy should be at the heart of this ongoing conversation, where children learn through active participation in the school system and syllabus development, and young people are helped to understand themselves and wider society through this process.

There is one area of democracy over which the Scottish Parliament has no powers and that is industrial democracy. The advantages of having ways of governing enterprises that are open and democratic are numerous and many of the world's most successful companies already have strong industrial democracy. Ideally, trade unions would have the right to negotiate terms and conditions for employees at an industry sector level, workers would have the right to elect representatives onto company boards, and joint and mutual management committees would help manage the 'shop floor'. Scotland has no power to legislate for these things but it might be possible to explore some kind of 'kitemark' system for recognising good practice in industrial democracy. The Scottish Government and local authorities could also ensure that it implements the best possible practise on trade union and workers rights. It is a weak alternative to real power to change employment relations, but it is all that can be done.

In the end democracy relies on its citizens, just like an economy relies on its labour force. There's no question that much time and effort has been put into identifying whether education is fit for purpose in preparing people for their lives as employees or business leaders. Over recent decades it is certainly possible to argue that less effort has been put into making education fit for purpose in preparing people for their lives as citizens. The direction in which we should move our education system to focus on producing happy, confident, able and well-rounded citizens is explored in chapter 11. In all thinking about education it is essential never to forget that, certainly, education is vital for wellbeing as well as national prosperity. But we should never forget that education is also central to democracy. The Democracy Academy should play a major role in curriculum development for citizenship, and the democratic role of schools should be emphasised at all times.

Democracy is often messy, because humans, communities and societies are messy, inconsistent, and complicated. Corporatism is often neat, because corporate structures and bureaucracies are generally simple and consistent. But it wasn't democracy that invaded Iraq or encouraged the conditions which caused a global financial crisis. You can't just abolish the people. So you either better put them in charge or expect disillusion with government and the state to rise further—until something gives.

Chapter Eight
Providing for the Common Weal

Our common weal requires us to have good jobs, prosperity through high wages, the useful goods and services we need, the innovation to create new useful products, and the ability to build great infrastructure. This is generally called 'the economy' and its purpose should be to provide for the common weal. Chapter three explored what that economy would look like and explained why we would require an industrial policy to get there.

The primary aims are to rebalance the economy: away from a routine service sector to high-value-added service and manufacturing; away from extremes in pay between top and bottom to greater pay equality; away from male and female experiences of work to a gender-desegregated labour market; away from profit-extraction to high-value productivity; away from short-term speculation to long-term investment. This should be done by rejecting the assumption that a 'let them do as they please' approach will deliver this. There must be collective intervention and we must recognise that we need effective action across all the relevant policy behaviours. That means all partners must be actively engaged: enterprises, trade unions, national government, local government, government agencies, and communities. It is this mutual model which has made the Nordic and German economies so effective. And in part, that is because they take both a national and a sector-level approach.

First, let us consider national approaches. There is very little evidence that it is possible to stimulate a substantial increase in productive economic activity (particularly manufacturing but also high-value service) by tweaking macro-level policies (which just means policies such as interest rates and tax which affect the whole economy at the same time). Indeed, because some of the macro-level policies that you might want to put in place to encourage manufacturing would emphasise long term investment over speculation, they would be against the interests of the financial industries and so are unlikely to happen. In any case, none of these powers (other than some relatively minor elements of business taxation) are ones Scotland can control. So if we are to see substantial change at a national level, there will need to be active intervention.

National Service Companies

To do this, we must identify high-value industry sectors which can be directly stimulated by making a self-contained business case. There are two in particular for which an immediate business case can be produced: housing and energy. Let's begin with housing.

As is discussed at various points in this book, housing is an essential policy area for the transformation of Scotland. In everything from controlling the harmfully high price of housing to desegregating social classes to creating better social environments for people to reducing CO_2 emissions to producing high-pay manufacturing jobs, housing is essential. It also has a self-contained business model. The management and design of new housing developments is considered in chapter 11, along with the need to free people from the excessive costs of housing. The means of building these houses is through long-term borrowing arrangements with a Scottish National Investment Bank.

Perhaps the most effective model for this is to create a National Mutual Company, the National Housing Company. This would build a new generation of first-rate public rental housing. The company would borrow against rents over a 30 year period. This would enable rents to be lower than now when borrowing is done over shorter periods (and if combined with very active planning and tax policies designed to reduce the cost of land, rents could be lower still). Therefore subject to available land, the company could be entirely demand-led—just like in the 1950s, anyone could put their name down on a list for a public rental house and so long as they'd commit to say five years of renting, as many houses could be built as there are names on the list.

The benefits of doing this through a national company are many: the ability to improve efficiency through scale; removing the profit-maximising, wealth-extracting imperative commercial developers currently impose; greatly improving the technologies of housebuilding in Scotland and therefore the environmental performance of housing; or creating much higher quality jobs in construction. A national company should build German-style 'house factories' in which high-tech housing is built on a production line and assembled quickly and efficiently where they are to be built. The jobs created are not labouring jobs but skilled jobs in design, engineering, and construction—as well as the traditional trades. And as the financial model is not limited to those able to raise finance for the costly business of deposits and mortgages on Britain's over-priced housing, so demand should be substantial.

A National Housing Company would also have an important role in renovating the existing housing stock. The financial model for this involves the company borrowing against the future savings in energy resulting from the renovation. Homeowners who want to improve their housing can commit to a fixed-price energy deal with the company. Once the work is completed the price of energy used by the house will fall substantially as insulation and the efficiency of heating systems is improved. The gap between the fixed energy price and the reduced cost of energy actually used creates an income stream for the company, as well as maintaining the fabric of the building, reducing long run costs and thus tackling fuel poverty. It can then borrow against this income stream to fund the initial work. In this way families can have substantially improved housing quality and Scotland can reduce CO_2 emissions with no additional cost to either.

By creating high-quality rental housing and by stimulating the improvement of existing properties, the National Housing Company would create substantial amounts of economic activity which the current market simply isn't—and these are high- and medium-skill jobs in a productive sector. There is little or no cost to the public purse in any of this and the economic returns are immediate. Over time, it would reduce our over-investment in low quality housing and generate a surplus for continuous investment in homes which are fit for purpose.

The same model can be used to create a National Energy Company, which would have two important functions. One is to begin to bring the energy system in Scotland back into collective ownership (this is considered further in chapter nine). The other is to capture for Scotland much more of the manufacturing and design employment which should come along with Scotland having some of the most impressive natural assets for renewable energy generation in Europe.

The current model is an economic disaster for Scotland. Private developers (often foreign-owned) are granted permission to erect energy-generating infrastructure. They then do this on land that they buy or by renting land from large private landowners. They then import the technologies to generate the energy from overseas manufacturers and erect them, often using short-term agency labour. From that point onwards they harvest the energy generation tariffs from the government and the energy corporations. The developer gets rich, the landowner gets rich, the overseas company that makes the technology gets rich— and Scotland gets some temporary jobs in erection and then a smaller number of jobs in maintenance. It is an incredibly generous way for the commons to provide its energy needs, gifting most of the economic benefit to wealthy individuals and corporations.

A National Energy Company can change these economics. First it can borrow from the National Investment Bank against the future revenues which come from the electricity which will be generated. This will then allow the company to operate on publicly-owned property or purchase any land or other rights necessary to build the generating infrastructure. Once this is installed, the profit it is generating will return to the company and not be exported to developers who are often based overseas.

Another crucial difference is that a National Energy Company can choose where to source its technology from—and can choose Scotland. As well as installing technology, a National Energy Company would be a manufacturing business which builds the technology and a national research centre which would develop the next generations of energy technology. It is that next generation of technologies where the opportunity for developing a substantial export business opens up. It also enables it to do things the current market is not—in particular, installing substantial amounts of energy storage. The need for energy storage is discussed in chapter nine, but the potential economic impact of designing, building, and installing energy storage technology in Scotland now is enormous.

As well as electricity generation, the National Energy Company should look at large- and medium-scale heat generation. Working closely with the National Housing Company, it can build and install district heating systems (where one boiler serves an entire block of houses or flats via insulated piping, greatly improving efficiency). It should also be involved in exploring next generation heating technologies such as heat recovery from disused mining infrastructure or inter-seasonal heat-store, where large heat stores collect solar heat in the summer months and then store it for use over the winter months.

This business model faces some substantial problems and uncertainties, mostly deriving from the UK Government's attacks on the funding models for renewable energy—which hit Scotland hardest. However, as the economic viability of new technologies improve, it can only be hoped that a viable renewable energy sector in Scotland, and a substantial national company which creates large numbers of jobs in the high-skill manufacturing sector and installs substantially greater amounts of energy storage will be possible.

Again, all of these are economic benefits which the current market are denying Scotland. The combination of a planned approach to housing and energy could bring with it additional benefits: zero-carbon homes that actually export energy to the grid for most of the year are now as cheap as traditional social housing, and a coordinated housing and energy effort reveal obvious rewards, economically and environmentally.

These are two businesses which can rapidly create high-quality jobs in Scotland with very little public investment. However, they are both in industry sectors which are dominated by male employment. There is an ongoing debate about how best to address the problem of the gap in pay between men and women, much of that gap caused by gender segregation in the workforce (female employment tends to be concentrated in low pay sectors such as retail and care, while high pay sectors such as manufacturing and 'professional' careers tend to be dominated by men). In the long term, the aim should be to desegregate employment with gender no longer being an indicator of likely employment (this is discussed further in chapter ten). However, this will not address female low pay in the short term. As Scotland has no control over pay policy, this will need to be done through direct intervention.

One effective way to do this would be through a National Childcare Company. This would borrow against future contracts for childcare from the Scottish Government and use that to invest in infrastructure and a long-term business model, creating more high-skilled childhood practitioner jobs in the growing profession. This would vitally increase the number of staff in early education, and improve opportunities and wellbeing for those already in the sector—populated overwhelmingly by women. It would also be an opportunity for those in the sector to redesign the integration of their service into other areas of care (for example with health visitors and early years care in the NHS), and should create opportunities for practitioners to develop professionally, for example using their invaluable university research training in Academies. Increased salaries might not stem from 'professionalisation' alone, and increasing pay rates (perhaps by standardising hourly rates for the service) should be a primary policy goal of this proposal (see discussion of gender equality in chapter 10).

This would have more legal problems than the examples above (housing and energy are deregulated markets and so since they're not considered core government activity, they would not need to be 'on the books' or abide by procurement rules). Childcare might fall under procurement rules and so it is possible that rather than a National Childcare Company this would need to be done through local authorities. But interventions not only to create more high-pay jobs but crucially more high-pay jobs for women must be a priority.

Local Enterprise

Two other linked areas where there are very substantial opportunities for interventions to stimulate nationwide economic activity are in food production and the small and medium scale manufacturing sector. In both cases Scotland has enormous potential and in both cases there are similar barriers to achieving that potential.

In food and drink, Scotland has a globally recognised reputation for quality. It also has much more potential for supplying Scotland with homegrown and locally-produced food. One of the models which demonstrates this potential is the remarkable success of the Scottish craft brewery industry. Beginning with very little, Scotland now has a booming industry made up of small, locally-owned brewing companies producing high-quality beers which are sold successfully to Scottish customers. This is high-skill work and involves effective and often local supply chains.

This model can be replicated in other areas such as artisan bread baking, cheese-making, and a range of other craft food making. But beyond this, there is also the scope for many more small and medium-scale farmers and other food producers (from game to seafood to cured meats) to sell quality food products directly to Scottish customers, and to export high value products. This can produce substantial economic benefit to rural areas but also opens up opportunities in craft food processing right across the country (and new technologies such as developments in assisted growing using grow-lights can extend both seasonal and geographic availability).

This same model of small-to-medium disaggregated businesses in high-value production applies to design and manufacture. Scotland is a design-rich country with world-class art schools and universities. There is already a developing design and small manufacturing sector in Scotland. It is producing everything from clothing to furniture to technology to household goods. It is also working to develop good connections and effective supply chains. Technological developments mean that the economics of micro-, small- and medium-scale manufacture are viable (computer-controlled technologies enable activities at a small scale which once would only have been possible in a large factory). And the quality of Scottish-designed products is high, creating desirable consumer goods.

These two sectors create exactly the kind of economic activity that Scotland should aspire to. It is high-skill and high-quality. It is dominated by large numbers of small businesses with strong ethical values, good employment relationships, and comparatively high pay. Many of them can operate in a disaggregated way, meaning any place—rural or urban, small town or city—can aim to develop a thriving local economy in these modern industries. They generally have good environmental performance, encourage consumers to buy quality which lasts, are highly innovative, and have very substantial growth potential, including in international export markets. They make Scotland an even more attractive destination for tourists and within these businesses are visionary (and often young) designers, manufacturers, and managers who, if we can keep them and help them grow their businesses, offer great promise for Scotland's future economy and society. And they capture all of their economic value in the Scottish economy, for the Scottish economy.

But both face similar barriers. The strategy of 'let them do as they please' actively rigs the market against these industries. In effect the means of distribution (the shops in which you can buy these types of goods) are a cartel which controls what goods people have access to and what price will be paid to producers and manufacturers. The ideological theory behind this is that these big cartel players are inherently more efficient because of their size. And they are efficient, but the benefits of that efficiency do not always flow to customers as much as to shareholders— and the price of efficiency is almost always borne by the producers.

To take one example, there have been occasions on which Scottish potato growers have been paid five pence per kilo for their produce. This has then been sold in supermarkets within an hour of where they were grown (transport costs being very little) for £1 a kilo. The position of milk producers is well known. But we may not be aware the extent to which imported goods force Scottish goods out of the market, not because they are cheaper or better but because it suits the economics of supermarkets. This is both effectively monopsony (an economic term which refers to a market where there is only one buyer who can dictate the price paid to producers) and can be close to monopoly (a market where there is only one seller who can dictate the terms to customers). Which means that the vast majority of the national means of sourcing and distributing food has been left in the hands of four supermarket corporations—and similar problems are encountered in other areas of retail.

So by far the biggest barrier to the development of these sectors is that they are locked out of the market for domestic customers and are forced to market themselves as niche or specialist and cannot easily achieve a high street presence. Allowing the access to Scotland's consumer markets to be so overwhelmingly controlled in ways which harm Scotland's manufacturing sector is not wise. To tackle this Scotland could set up a National Distribution and Export Company to help small producers in the logistics of achieving the benefits of critical mass which would enable them to compete fairly and on an even playing field with corporations.

Such a company would need to be highly innovative in how it is designed and in how it addresses the problems of market access. One approach might be to develop very efficient Scotland-wide delivery systems linked to online ordering. If there was a rapid, affordable home delivery network designed specifically to support domestic manufacturing and food production it would rapidly increase the size of market for these producers. Another might be to develop 'hub shops'. These would be open-access facilities in every town where producers could bring their produce and products for sale. Each producer could be identified by a barcode on products. Shoppers would simply put products in their basket like in any supermarket and as they were scanned at the checkout the price of the goods would be transferred straight to producers' bank accounts (minus a fee to cover the running of the shop). Subject to quality standards, anyone could become a registered supplier which means that cottage industries could develop. There may be other even more innovative means of getting Scottish goods to Scottish customers, and we must explore these options to grow these industries.

Another area where critical mass would help is in accessing export markets. Already small suppliers have to turn down export orders because while the order may be very substantial for the producer, they are just too small to make the economics of exporting viable. If exporting can be done not on the basis of individual producers but on the basis of syndicates of producers organised through a national export company, it should be possible to make those export markets viable—and in so doing, more Scottish suppliers currently exporting through deals with intermediaries could develop direct exporting links of their own.

A second factor where collective intervention could make a substantial difference is in the provision of processing facilities. Many small and medium producers struggle to expand because of the barrier of infrastructure. They may require access to facilities, but not such that they are able to make the full investment on their own. For example, if a Scottish apple grower wished to juice all of the apples produced, it could afford to do it via very small-scale equipment that would make the task very time-consuming and inefficient, or via a large facility which it might only use for one or two days a year. And yet a mobile processing facility can be built on a lorry which could serve many growers across the nation over the course of a season, making the economics viable again. There are already wonderful examples of open access, shared manufacturing facilities and they are already making a difference—but they are insufficient to stimulate the scale of expansion this sector is capable of. The job of providing this 'right size' infrastructure should be given to Scotland's economic development agencies and to local authorities, which should create this infrastructure according to local demand, the scope for developing local industries, and the potential for future industries in the region.

Similar support could be offered collectively by economic development agencies to help achieve critical mass on the services (particularly the legal and financial services) which these types of businesses need. The process of securing protection for intellectual property, trademark protection, and patents can be complex, expensive, and time-consuming. Big companies have in-house legal teams which deliver services such as these and this gives them a substantial advantage over smaller competitors. Again, collective provision can level the playing field and enable smaller businesses to compete.

A final area where collective public intervention might make a substantial difference is in software development—and in particular, open source software development. This is a crucial and rapidly-expanding aspect of software development and Scotland could do much to increase its software industry sector if it focussed on promoting practices which increase the market for open source software expertise. The easiest way to do this would be to gradually change the IT systems of all public authorities to open source. This would create new opportunities for Scottish-based developers to enable this move for government systems (increasing the amount of expertise in this area Scotland sources from within Scotland), and would also stimulate the development of expertise in this field. Scotland could be an open source leader and public authorities could stimulate that leadership role.

In all the cases given above and in many more, Scotland should be pursuing a strategy of 'smart specialisation'. This simply means seeking to identify specialised areas where Scotland is particularly good and seeking to be the best in those areas. This means producing particularly innovative companies. There is much which can be done to promote this kind of economy-wide innovation such as effective links between small businesses and universities. But one very effective thing Scotland can do is to embed design education in the heart of the school curriculum. Design approaches (looking at how things work and seeing how they can be made to work better for the people who need them) create the capacity to pursue smart specialisation. This should be a discipline all Scottish school children are exposed to throughout their school careers and has the potential to help generations of citizens become more analytical, innovative, and adaptable in their changing environments.

This represents six industry sectors where Scotland could achieve very substantial growth and high-quality employment by making collective intervention to achieve things that market alone simply aren't achieving. But there are other areas that could be considered. Tourism in Scotland may not be as well-served by overseas promotion as it might be. Domestically, more could be done to encourage tourism within Scotland. For example, local councils could be tasked with producing very local tourism 'offers' to market towns and villages as destinations for day trips and longer stays. Encouraging more domestic tourism would have substantial benefits, not least in creating better year-round utilisation of the tourism infrastructure we have. Improving quality through training and support would be another useful intervention.

As outlined previously in this book, there are many reasons to support a Land Value Tax but one of the most important is to align the value of land much more closely to its economic value (which means the value that can be earned from the productive use of the land). If land is more expensive than any profit that can be made from its productive, use it will remain a speculative investment or preserved for 'country sports'. A strategy for developing land-based industries based around the introduction of a Land Value Tax should be considered. Similarly, serious thought should be given to developing a marine industry strategy, looking at everything from the development of kelp farming to attempting to bring some of the benefits of a rapidly-developing Arctic trading route to the north of Scotland.

Sector Associations

These are all areas where there are market failures (or in the case of tourism some necessary collective interventions). They could all deliver substantial benefits if there is national action. However there has been a long-standing aversion to what economic development professionals would call 'picking winners' (which basically just means putting all of your eggs in very few baskets). This aversion is partly questionable and closely tied to me-first theories which are based on the doctrine of 'let them do as they please'. But it is certainly not entirely wrong, and focussing our entire economic strategy at a small number of sectors would be unwise. Indeed, there is a strong case to be made against neglecting any industry sectors.

To explain why this is, it's worth thinking about the Nordic timber industries. In the recent past these were traditional logging industries, cutting down trees to make planks. But because the industry constantly looked at ways to develop and innovate, it has now become one of the world's leading advanced timber materials industries, producing advanced plywood products which can be almost as strong as steel for structural engineering. This is an industry which many countries would have considered old, routine, and not worth bothering about. But it shows precisely why making these assumptions is harmful.

In fact there is a strong case for Scotland adopting an economic development strategy of 'no sector left behind'; working from the assumption that no form of economic activity isn't capable of improving, innovating, and creating new products, markets, and approaches. That requires us to reject both 'magic button' approaches (using only a limited set of macro-level policies) and the entire 'let them do as they please' philosophy. But it also requires a genuine sector-level mutual development approach.

The solution to this is to allow industry sectors to produce their own economic development strategies in a mutual way and working with the full range of government and its agencies. This should be done by assisting in the establishment of sector associations. These would be loosely constituted groups which provide a space where all the players in an industry sector can come together and discuss the best approaches to development in an open, mutual, and creative way. They would involve small business, big business, supply chains businesses, trade unions, employees, education and training providers, communities (where industries are geographically based), and consumers or service users (where appropriate).

It would be the job of these sector associations to identify the full set of factors which would influence their business environment in ways that encourage the most positive development. The role of economic development professionals and representatives of government and its agencies would be to support this process and provide advice—but not to lead it (although government may very well wish to set goals and targets such as 'raise wages' or 'improve environmental performance'). Associations would be required to come to negotiated and consensual approaches, informed by the democratic mechanisms explored in Academies, and not dominated by only one of the partners (certainly not dominated by whichever parts of an industry sector are best able to pay for lobbyists). This consensus approach would form a sector development plan.

It would then be the responsibility of the different players identified in a development plan to enact their part of the plan. Some of this will be internal, for example enterprises asking supply chain companies to behave in slightly different ways, or employees seeking more training and development. Some of it will be external, for example asking local authorities to alter procurement policies, or asking development agencies to assist with export support. The aim is to coordinate as much action as is felt necessary across as many partners as are required to deliver that policy. This will create sector-specific industrial policies. Of course, sector associations cannot bind others to the proposals they produce (democratically elected governments must have the final say in public policy), but it should be possible to produce genuinely powerful development strategies through mutual working.

A sector association approach will have three major benefits. First, it draws on the knowledge, experience and creativity of a wider group of partners through the mutual development process. Second, solutions will be tailored to the sector and the sector will have to take responsibility for it's own development. And thirdly, it will help to respond to the problem of different levels of development within and between different industry sectors, bolstering and supporting adaptable and innovative sectors across Scotland.

It is important to note that many of the elements of an 'industrial policy toolkit' that an ideal Scotland would be able to use are ones over which Scotland has no power—in particular industrial democracy, business taxes (including VAT), and regulatory powers. However, this does not mean there is nothing left in the toolkit. For example: a Scottish National Investment Bank and a municipal banking sector, incentives to 'anchor' companies in Scotland and discourage equity sell-out, influencing land values, reforming public procurement to create stable order books (and innovative purchasing practice), export support, distribution and market access support, provision of intermediary infrastructure, more support for different ownership models (such as cooperatives and mutuals), integrated access to university and college expertise, collective management of patents and intellectual property, establishment of research hubs, conditionality in licensing of access to natural resources, careers guidance, sector diversification agencies, conditionality on state support, adopt 'use it or lose it' approaches (compulsory purchasing where development of assets is being blocked), changing best value criteria—and more.

An economy is there to provide for a society's common weal. It is society's responsibility to make sure that it does.

Chapter Nine
In our hands, by our hands

Me-first politics thrives on insecurity, on dependence. It creates
systems where citizens, consumers, communities, democracies and
nations are supplicant to big business. It has achieved this by creating
a 'naked society', one in which many of our sources of security have
been taken from us and sold to private interests, where the fundamental
fabric of our lives is largely controlled not by us in our interests but
by big business in its interests. Our energy system is a patchwork of
private business interests, our telecommunications network is nothing
more than a marketplace of private big business, housing supply is
driven almost wholly by private profit motive, our trains and buses are
owned by corporations and run for their profit, and our airports are
not our airports but are private airports. Our food distribution system
is more like a private cartel, our money supply system is wholly owned
by a banking system that virtually no-one really trusts—even our
public spaces (from shopping malls to schools to hospitals to previously
publicly-owned land) are being privatised or redesigned for private
interests. This is 'rentier capitalism': a form of capitalism where you make
money not from productivity but from buying up essential assets and
services and then use a kind of monopoly control over them to extract
greater profits from customers.

Heat, power, communication, housing, transport, food, money
and space—could anything be more fundamental to our security and
wellbeing? So why are they designed to extract profit from us, some of
which they then use to pay political lobbyists to make sure that there is
no democratic interference with their profit-making (unless, of course,
they require one of those frequent bail-outs). It's almost like our whole
society is dressed up in clothes that it doesn't own, that it must rent, that
someone else can take away at any time.

This is all done in the name of 'market efficiency'. And yet, again
and again, we've seen publicly or collectively owned alternatives
delivering better service and better efficiency. In truth the impact of
this was not an exceptional improvement in service—as we can see

by looking at other countries which kept these services in collective ownership and have seen substantially better improvements in the performance of the same services. The main impact has been to transfer large amounts of money from general populations to corporations. It is this mechanism which has played such a big part in making Britain such an unequal country.

No-one should want to retreat into a closed-off world in which we do not cooperate effectively across borders and across the world. But it is not wrong of a government—of a society—to ensure its own security. It is not wrong to want to be more self-sufficient, and less exposed to every up and down of geopolitics (should our energy always get more expensive because of someone else's war?). It is important for people's wellbeing, for shared prosperity, for a much more even process of economic development (where wealth is generated all over a nation and not just in its financial hubs where they trade commodities and finance), and for real environmental sustainability. It is not wrong to believe that our collective wellbeing should be in our hands and that it should be assured by our hands.

Of course, Scotland has few powers in this area. Ideally we should own our own national grid (Britain is the only country in Europe that doesn't). Trains and buses should be owned and run for public benefit. National infrastructure should be planned and owned nationally. But Scotland does not have the powers to renationalise, nor the powers to finance it (and any new powers Scotland can expect in this area appear to be limited). But this does not mean that we cannot take much more of our security into our own hands.

Energy

In chapter eight the scope for taking greater collective control over energy generation through a National Energy Company was discussed. In addition to this, it is possible for the proposed regional councils to create municipal energy supply companies. Every regional council could set up a company to sell electricity (and gas) to customers in their council area. By in effect creating a council-wide syndicate of citizens to bulk-purchase energy, it is possible not only to ensure democratic control over energy supply but also to reduce energy costs (profits would not be taken from customers to give to shareholders). Any profits made would be used to improve public services, or reduce local taxes. This would link collective control of a greater proportion of energy generation with greater collective control over energy supply to customers, and would therefore begin to provide greater security of energy supply and greater price security for energy users.

In addition Scotland has the potential to create heating systems which can do much more to help us become self-sufficient in heating needs and less reliant on imported gas. Some of the technologies for this are still developing (such as inter-seasonal heat store where solar thermal energy is stored over the summer for use over the winter). Others are much better developed (such as biomass where Scotland has potentially enormous land resources which could be used to create wood pellets for biomass boilers). These kinds of systems should be built into new housing developments as district heating (where a block or entire street can be fed from one large and super-efficient boiler, with houses metered for hot water use). They can also be retrofitted. The National Energy Company should be tasked with developing plans for innovating Scotland's heating infrastructure.

Housing

We've also seen how greater security can be achieved in housing supply through a National Housing Company. It is important to be clear that this policy is not only about security for those who rent one of the new houses, but for much of the housing market. Housing in Britain has been used as a means of financial speculation and has pushed house prices up to unsustainable levels. At the moment thousands of homeowners in Scotland have mortgages that would be unaffordable if it was not for historically low interest rates (and many people are struggling with housing costs even at those low rates). If interest rates rise, many people may lose their houses to the banks. A National Housing Company should develop plans for a mortgage-to-rent scheme. If people are at risk of losing their house they can convert their mortgage into rent by selling their house to the housing company which would then refinance the housing and rent it back to the same family at a rate more affordable than the mortgage payments. The family would have a life-long right to keep that house and adapt and develop it as if it was theirs. And they will have housing security.

Another important way that the housing company would create better housing security would be by controlling house price rises. Rising house prices are both a major social problem (housing insecurity, poor quality of house design and build, cost of living, inability of younger generation to get access to housing) and a major economic problem (driving inequality, acting as a drag on innovation as employees are 'trapped' in specific jobs and locations by mortgages, exposing the economy to very substantial risk of housing bubbles and crashes). Over the last 20 years in Germany, house prices have not risen at all in real terms and this is an important part of their economic and social success. In fact, one of the reasons me-first politicians give for not building public rental housing is that it would slow down house price rises and reduce the ability of property speculators to make money on housing bubbles. A substantial increase in housing supply in the public rental sector would have a real impact on rising house prices, stabilising the housing market and creating better security for everyone.

The low supply of high-quality rental in Scotland also means that rental costs are often either too high, too insecure, or the properties of insufficient quality—or all three. To address this a proper system of rent control should be put in place. A simple proposal for rent controls is to base the levels of rent on the council tax bands, but since the last assessment of property value for council tax bands in Scotland was over twenty years ago, a new system is required, as highlighted in chapter 6.

Fairer systems already exist elsewhere: in the Netherlands, an independent panel rates properties in a points system based on size, location, condition, and local amenities, and sets rates accordingly. A rent commission allows renters to challenge the level of rent set. Any increase in rent is announced annually by the government, in the same way that an increase (or decrease) in public-sector pay is announced.

We then must improve security of tenure. The normality of a six-month lease in the UK, where a landlord can then kick you out without providing any other reason for doing so than that they want to, is abnormal in most of Europe. Instead, a tenant's tenure should not have any contract time limit, in the same way as someone who gets a mortgage doesn't, with the flexibility to leave at any point providing they've paid the month's rent and kept to all the conditions of their contract. Tenants would be informed before any changes to their rent at the annual rate setting so they can decide whether they want to stay on or not. If the landlord decides they do not want them for whatever reason and this is contested by a tenant, the rent commission would decide whether the landlord has viable grounds for making them leave their home. Not only does this create greater security for the tenant, but the landlord also knows what rent their going to receive over a longer time period and can plan ahead.

Housing has been created as a system for generating profit, not providing people with housing security. This can and should be reversed using such ideas.

Local banking

Another essential aspect of our lives where we can give people the option of choosing collective security is in banking. There is little love for Britain's banking system and the endless tales of mis-selling and corrupt practice are wearyingly familiar.

But the extent to which retail banking has pressed us to take up more borrowing and bigger and bigger mortgages is perhaps the most damaging role they have taken. Add to this the poor track record of the private banking sector in providing finance to small business, which barely improved even after banks were given public money to improve their lending rates. That this lending isn't the kind of long term, supportive lending that productive start-up companies need compounds the issue.

Many countries have retail banking sectors dominated by municipal banking: mutual banking organised regionally across the country in democratic ways with a non-commercial purpose. It offers a large proportion of retail banking in Germany and Japan and there is no reason Scotland could not move towards that kind of model. Just as every regional council could set up an energy company, so they can set up a municipal development bank (a number already have them, but the model is not generally the one that should be followed so they're referred to here as municipal or local development banks).

If a banking system of this sort existed right across Scotland then those banks, working with the National Investment Bank, could collectively capitalise themselves using local authority pension funds and collectively promote themselves to households and businesses—but only within their own region. This could be an attractive proposition for 'savers' to put their money into as commercial rates of interest for savers is low unless they invest in higher risk financially engineered 'products', while local businesses are crying out for stable long-term finance.

It would therefore be guaranteed that pension fund investment locally would go towards regional development, with the development bank working closely with local credit unions and other community-based financial institutions. This principle of regional investment would hopefully encourage more people to move away from the big commercial banks and set-up their account with their regional development bank, which would provide a significant further basis for investment in regional development. While there are different models of how these could be delivered, they could use existing council premises to create face-to-face banking services wherever there is a council presence. This would create an extensive network of banking facilities. But as more and more banking is done online or using new technology, much of the infrastructure would be virtual.

These banks would be governed democratically, with those who sign-up with the bank able to vote at the AGM. They would have different values and priorities to the existing private banks. They would be driven by the welfare of their customers. They would of course provide loans to people who need them—but they wouldn't constantly pester customers with expensive advertising encouraging them to take out loans they don't need, and they would not provide rates of interest which exploit the precariousness of low-pay and zero-hours contracts as do payday loan companies and some credit-providing shops that target those on low pay. Instead people could come to their regional bank and work out a low-interest loan with a long-term payment plan, as long as there was a realistic means by which the loan could be re-paid.

The local development banks would see a successful relationship with their business customers as the long-term growth and development of those businesses and not on the basis of how quickly they can get a profit back. They would be part of 'anchoring strategies' that would seek the continued presence of businesses in communities through loan conditionality (the loan being on the basis of a business continuing to invest in that community or region) and equity finance (the local bank taking a stake in the business to ensure its long-term strategy and vote at AGMs). And the decision-making on business loans would not be a tick-box exercise as to whether a business meets a pre-defined list of requirements, but would be based on local knowledge and understanding. Overall this might make these banks less profitable than their private competitors, but since they're not trying to generate profit for shareholders, they don't need to be. They just need to be the good, functional, supportive banks our society needs.

This is an ambitious initial proposal for how regional councils could create more security by providing citizens with collective opportunities to access essential services. However, in future there are other possible services it might be worth considering treating in the same way. For example, short of being able to nationalise the provision of broadband access and the telephone network (which would put the planning of proper broadband roll-out back in democratic hands), broadband and telecom services could be offered by municipal companies on a no-profit basis.

Food

The position of food has already been partly considered. Creating food hubs and distribution systems will enable us to get more Scottish produce to more Scottish customers and so make us somewhat less reliant on imports (and will also improve the economics of the food production industry to ensure its greater sustainability). We should also sustain and support local food production by using public procurement policy. Schools, hospitals, and other public bodies should integrate procurement horizontally, with different bodies within a city or region working together. They could construct contracts for food supply in ways which best enable local suppliers to win those contracts, including making them smaller in size and applying conditions that favour local suppliers wherever possible. Whenever considering food security it is important to be aware that national and global food security is not the same thing as household food security—households in food-rich nations may themselves be food-poor, an issue explored further in chapter 10.

As part of a national plan to make Scotland more food sovereign, a National Policy Academy looking at food and agricultural policy and practice might be set up, covering other issues such as rural economy too. This could help support professional development for farmers in a shift towards agroecology to produce as much food as now, but by working smarter with nature, and moving away from mainstream aggressive farming techniques, which can cause more harm in the long term. This would involve investment in extension services which transfer knowledge in both directions and help farmers deliver environmental and social goods as well as commodities. It could also support cooperation between farmers, and between farmers and communities, and aim to accelerate opportunities for new farmers to get access to land and start-up capita—providing they farm using innovative techniques. It would seek to encourage a shift from 'food as a commodity' to 'food for people'.

Transport

Another area that demands serious consideration for future planning is transport. Scotland's transport infrastructure falls well behind its continental comparators. In fact, there is a strong argument to say that by the time Scotland put in enough investment to catch up with the European norm on transport infrastructure, Europe would have moved on and we'd be as far behind as before. This is a crucial area where we should take a 'nextgen' strategy: recognise that to catch up with best practice we need to skip a generation of technology, and thus approach and start planning for the one that comes after that.

A Transport Policy Academy should be established, in the open and participative model as is the case with these Academies (as discussed in chapter six). It should immediately be tasked with producing a major report on possible transport models for the next generation of transport in Scotland. There are many questions it would want to consider. How do we transition to electric transport and what infrastructure is needed? What transport requirements would Scotland need if it achieved a more disaggregated economy with much more robust local economies? What does the future of city centre transport look like and how should it work? Can Scotland greatly improve its use of marine transport and what would that mean? How can we strengthen international transport links?

In all of this, the role of reducing climate change emissions from the transport system would be central, as well as the role of transport in strengthening communities and reducing the reliance on private cars for mobility. The potential for economic impact through capturing any viable technology development and manufacture in Scotland would also be a particular focus.

Possible outcomes might include a vision of our cities replacing buses with driverless cars coordinated via mobile devices, or using some of the health budget to develop comprehensive and safe cycling infrastructure, as Copenhagen achieved in the 70s and 80s. It might include substantial investment in creating car charging infrastructure across Scotland. It might include an investment in overseas shipping links, or ways to better connect the Scottish islands to the wider economy, or inexpensive municipal car rental services to reduce the need to own a car. The aim would be to have this in place and then to develop it as a more detailed plan in time for the following parliamentary term.

In developing a self-reliant society, we must also consider who leads our biggest institutions and how they are led. There is a good case for exploring if there are barriers to a greater number of the leading roles in Scottish life being filled by people educated in Scotland. This was a controversial issue when it was raised during Scotland's referendum campaign, and asking why so many of Scotland's institutions are managed by people who were recruited from outside of Scotland was attacked for being 'parochial' or borderline racist. This is an entirely unfair response to a perfectly reasonable question; it is not insular for a nation to want to produce generations of people capable of great leadership from within its population. A comprehensive study should be undertaken to explore structural problems either in education, career development, or institutional issues which hinder the long-term opportunities of those raised in Scotland. And of course this is not just about Scotland; we should aspire to be a nation which does indeed import great talent, but which exports it as well.

Scotland in a global context

A self-reliant nation is not a closed nation. To be a strong, sustainable nation capable of standing on its own two feet, Scotland needs immigration too. Immigration brings an enormous amount of benefit to a nation. It brings in innovation as people come from different cultural and industrial backgrounds. It strengthens and widens the existing national culture, enlivens our arts and our sport, and connects us to the world. Scots learn from immigration, gaining a greatly improved international perspective—and we still have much we can learn from second and third generation immigrants. Of course, Scotland has no powers over immigration. However, it does have the power to make the most of the immigration it has, and it should do this through promoting interculturalism. Interculturalism is based on the principle that all cultural experience becomes richer through the mixing and learning from different cultures, and encourages respectful cross-cultural dialogue to break down exclusive, self-segregation tendencies within every culture. In chapter ten a National Academy for Equality is proposed. This should be tasked with creating and disseminating practices which encourage and strengthen interculturalism. It could for instance look into why there are so few individuals from ethnic minorities working in Scottish media, analyse the dehumanisation of immigrants in public life, and look at what sort of community institutions could help bring people from diverse backgrounds into contact with one another to better understand and empathise with them. All of this would help make Scotland a better place for immigrants, and help immigrants make Scotland a better and stronger place.

There are also immigrants that have arrived in Scotland due to extreme circumstances in their country of origin. The indignities and challenges experienced in the asylum process are an omen for wider society. Underpinned by a culture of disbelief and where destitution is a policy tool, its genesis pre-dates Welfare Reform. The challenges faced by new refugees also serve as a forewarning—current systems and policy confirming and resigning them to immediate destitution and long term poverty. Refugee and asylum are also reserved matters, but here again, Scotland can lead by example by showing some compassion and humanity that is sadly lacking from the UK's approach.

As a result of the hostile political environment and inhumane asylum process, many have been led to focus on refugees' vulnerability at the expense of recognising resilience. We have the potential to learn from New Scots' resilience, benefit from their experience, and profit from their skills—if we enable them to participate in society. While recognising refugee resilience and ability to contribute as New Scots is vital, this resilience is futile if we don't work together to address structural and systems problems. Even the most resilient refugees require guidance and advocacy to negotiate systems; certain statutory services and rights—housing and benefits—are currently inaccessible to legitimate beneficiaries acting independently. There are already innovative approaches to tackling these issues in Scotland, including setting up 'mini-public' style consultation with refugees based on feedback, learning from the service, and wider policy issues. One basic policy might be ensuring asylum seekers are given a home up to the standard we'd expect of any Scottish citizen—a task for the new National Housing Company. Police Scotland could also refuse to cooperate with UK border agency 'dawn raids' on refugees and asylum seekers. Central to this is learning from each other: not only in adapting to best serve New Scots, but to enable New Scots to best integrate into Scottish society. These actions would at least be a sign that Scotland has a more inclusive and welcoming approach to some of the world's most vulnerable people.

These are areas where Scotland can take a specific approach to 'in our hands, by our hands'. Running through this and many of the proposals in the book is to see this concept of coherence and resilience at a national level also applied at a local level. We should aim to create communities which are better able to produce and consume local products. We should want to build an economy which brings life to the whole nation and to where people live, not one that relies wholly

on sucking people towards the cities. There are many occasions in
the book where the scope for producing virtuous circles of supply and
demand at a local level has been discussed, and the extent to which new
generations of economic activity can create durable and self-sufficient
economies where Scotland's populations already are. In some areas (such
as the broad range of land- and marine-based industries linked to better
transport and active housing policies), we could see the repopulation of
areas of Scotland which have suffered continuous population decline.
This in part means getting land into the hands of local people to make
productive use of it. Tenant farmers need to have the right to buy the
land from the lairds that own it. Community buy-outs need to be
made much easier. Government is almost always set in urban areas and
can have a tendency to see the world through urban eyes. Rural and
small-town Scotland often feels like it receives insufficient attention. A
localised strategy for our economy would begin to address that.

And in all of the above, the issue is most certainly not just Scotland's
security, but the world's. The world faces the incredibly serious issues
of climate change and its environmental and human impacts. One of
the factors which has driven this is the decline in these sustainable, local
economies, and the rise of transport and industrial emissions which
arise from the transnational production, processing, and distribution of
food and goods. Another is the inability to change many practices in
the wider economy which would improve environmental performance,
largely stemming from lack of democratic control. In everything from
the management of our land and environment, to the way transport
is organised and the impacts of our profit-driven housing market,
environmental impact too often appears to simply be an afterthought.
Scotland should contribute to the world's security by taking
responsibility for its own performance.

But we should also recognise that in having the highest
concentration of nuclear weapons in Europe, we also have a
responsibility to contribute to a continent- (and world-) wide debate
about nuclear disarmament. Of course, Scotland has no powers over
the area of defence, but this does not mean it can't lead education and
debate. In chapter ten it is proposed that there should be a National
Policy Academy focussed on violence reduction and conflict resolution

in a domestic context. However this Academy could also be tasked with raising awareness nationally and internationally about the need to move towards disarmament and new forms of global conflict resolution, looking at Scotland's international relations as well. Scotland might not have power over foreign affairs, but much of foreign affairs is about leading by example, and therefore all aspects of government—not just direct international development work—should operate on the principle of 'do no harm'. Me-first international relations is based on the principle of being seen to give with one hand, while secretly taking away with the other. Opposing trade policies which entrench me-first approaches in other countries is as important as doing so in Scotland.

Scotland should be open to the world, to be international in every sense. It's just a mistake to equate transnational corporations with internationalism. True, internationalism involves nations working together collectively to make us all stronger, more prosperous, and more secure—and of course more diverse and of richer culture. Being a good international citizen by taking responsibility for your own actions and challenging the harm done by the creation of the 'naked society' is not insular. It is forward-looking and responsible.

Chapter Ten
Putting All Of Us First

If Scotland is going to create a society that puts all of us first, it needs to deal with both poverty and inequality. But it must also be clear about what putting all of us first means. The me-first years didn't only affect the political right but heavily influenced parts of what had been the political left. Old concepts such as creating a society in which everyone was able to live a good life were replaced by new ones where the 'right thing to do' was simply to make it easier for anyone to fill the limited number of good lives available. Even now we hear the idea that the role of education is to let anyone from any social class have an equal chance of 'succeeding'. The implication seems to be that once that has been achieved, all those who 'fail' and suffer the consequences will somehow have 'deserved it'.

This is not putting all of us first. Of course economic or family background should not inhibit a child's chances of educational attainment. But nor should educational segregation replace social class segregation. Scotland should not be a country where your birth can condemn you to poverty—but nor should it become a country where your exam results can condemn you to poverty. It's not just that everyone should have an equal chance of 'playing the game'; it's that the game should not be rigged to hand riches to the winners and crumbs to the rest, and only within a narrow definition of what 'winning' even means.

Scotland faces two major tasks. The first is to create much greater equality. But this can't be done overnight, so the second is to tackle head-on the failures of inequality by tackling poverty and prejudice.

Tackling a low pay economy

The primary causes of economic inequality are all a result of the nature of the British (and global) economy. As has been discussed at length, we have an economy that emphasises extracting wealth from others rather than creating it, and which emphasises big transnational corporations over public utilities and independently owned smaller businesses. Along with the way the housing market has been managed as a speculative asset base and the way the financial sector has been transformed into a speculative venture, this has all created ways for a smaller number of people to extract a larger amount of wealth. That process creates few good jobs and so over time actually takes money away from average earners at the same time as giving very large amounts of money to those at the very top of the wealth spectrum.

The other enormously important factor in creating this inequality is the long-term weakening of industrial democracy and collective bargaining through trade unions. The ability of employees to fairly negotiate a larger proportion of the profits of a company being dedicated to wages has been crucial. The me-first evangelists claim that depressing wages is good for the economy because it increases profits. But profits are not good for the economy if they are used as a means to extract more and more wealth from that economy. Wages, on the other hand, remain in the economy and so are 'real national wealth'. The argument is also often made that paying fair wages makes businesses uncompetitive. However, where there is sector-level negotiation on wages then there is no competitive issue within the national economy, and since the de-unionised sectors are seldom in export businesses, they are not competing internationally.

Put bluntly, to achieve economic equality we need to increase wages. Some argue that this means we should allow the rich to get richer or that we need more rich people. This failed me-first vision of 'trickle down' is the opposite of what we need and the more it has been pursued as a policy, the greater inequality has grown. It is the failure of the whole income spectrum and not only one part of it that is the problem. It is the proportion of the working population in the income spectrum of less than (for example) £35,000 a year which drives inequality, representing four out of five working Scots.

It is hard to make direct comparisons between pay in different countries given different costs of living and so on. But it is possible to look at the spread—how many people there are at each level of pay. If you look at a successful country with low levels of poverty and inequality, not many people earn below a wage that in Scotland would be something like £25,000. However, in Scotland three out of five people earn less than £25,000. Meanwhile, most Nordic workers are in a wage category that in Scotland would look something like £25,000 to £35,000, while in Scotland it is only one in five. Nordic countries are successful not because of top pay or even average pay but because of a spread of wages across the economy that means most people are prosperous, able to pay tax, able to participate in the economy, and so on. So anyone who claims that Scotland can become better on the basis of more top-rate tax payers or more rich people does not understand why this has failed and is advocating the policy that caused the problem in the first place.

At this point, it is important to be clear that Scotland simply lacks the powers to address this fundamental problem in a systematic way. Scotland can't set a proper living wage, can't reinvest the massive benefit savings this would produce, and can't redesign tax credits to push wages up rather than down (tax credits should be seen as a subsidy to low-pay employers). Scotland can't alter any of the key macroeconomic levers which would create an environment in which it would be easier to rebalance the economy. Scotland can't touch any regulatory issues, any monetary policy issues, any major tax issues (it can't even influence National Insurance). And crucially it has no control over industrial democracy powers which have made Britain one of the developed economies with the worst workers' rights in the world.

In chapter eight a range of ways to directly stimulate the development of more high-pay jobs was explored. This will make a difference. A system of sector associations driving innovation in all parts of the economy will also help by using a wide range of powers such as procurement and investment. Building and creating a strong commons which invests in all of our lives will also be a significant contribution. But these strategies alone will be insufficient to make as much progress as should be made. Put simply, it will not be easy to achieve a more equal Scotland in an increasingly less equal Britain. This economic reality must be properly understood.

One thing the public sector should do is to set the rest of the economy a good example. There has been an expansion of the pay gaps in the public sector just as in the private sector and while these have not been as bad, there have been worrying signs. Alien concepts like a bonus culture have been used by those at the top of the public sector to increase their income. Governance mechanisms in many publicly-funded organisations do not appear to be capable of restraining executive pay which has not only risen well out of step with average pay but—despite public outrage—continues to do so. Democratic governance of institutions will help, but there should be a national 'road map' for the public sector which has the specific aim of narrowing the wage spectrum, restraining the pay of middle and senior management and setting an example of good practice for others.

It would be possible to look at a range of measures such as 'kitemarks' for businesses which have better pay and industrial democracy policies, or even some use of conditionality in public contracts or lending by municipal development banks to encourage better performance. Sector associations developing economic development strategies should be tasked to consider how employers can better contribute to greater equality, both economic and social. And all agencies involved in economic development should be given a specific socioeconomic obligation to develop the economy in such a way that it becomes more equal. However, while it is worth exploring these options, as mentioned before, we must be realistic in how much they alone can achieve.

Ending gender segregation in labour

One area where more must be achieved is the problem of gender pay inequality. This is largely a result of gender segregation in the labour market where female employment tends to concentrate around low pay industry sectors more than male employment as a whole. In chapter eight a possible intervention to address this problem immediately and directly was proposed by creating a National Childcare Service, creating more and better paid jobs for women (and particularly young women). This will make a difference but is not without its problems. In particular, there is a risk that moves such as this will in fact entrench gender segregation in the workforce, for example reinforcing the idea that caring is a 'female' responsibility. This risk is worth taking to do something immediately on female pay inequality, with more done to attract men to the increasingly professionalised sector.

In the long term the aim must be to do everything we can to change attitudes to what is 'male' work and what is 'female' work. There are few remaining jobs in which physical strength is a crucial aspect of work skills, and old stereotypes which may have played a part in putting women off considering some careers (or put off employers considering hiring women in these roles) have no place in modern society. The days when an 'engineer' was a man in an oily boiler suit have passed. Today an engineer is more likely to work with computer aided design, and the future of manufacture plants will be largely automated. In this we should avoid reifying assumptions that value typically 'masculine' fields such as science and maths as 'better' or more 'professional' than their 'feminine' counterparts: nursing is one of the most vital and valuable professions in our society, and we have all suffered from a lack of robust and better-funded cultural policy.

It is important that this is something that all school pupils understand at an early age, integrated into a reformed school curriculum which allows all children the flexibility to explore and engage in a wide variety of skills and trainings. To support this, we need a redesigned Personal and Social Education (PSE) syllabus which moves away from the grade-based careers advice which dominates the curriculum, and towards a more well-rounded and holistic approach to citizenship, human rights, and equalities. Young men and women should not think their lives are defined by the subjects they take in high school, and instead should leave secondary education having explored the myriad opportunities in the labour market and the mechanisms of inequality they may face—one of which may not be childcare if we have a national service in place.

Some of the other policies which would help in this goal are reserved to Westminster, for example mandatory reporting practices, regulation of working hours and working practices (making them more family-friendly), or regulatory quotas. Once again there may be some work-arounds and a gender equality and socioeconomic duties might be placed on economic development agencies. There is also a strong case for a consistent policy of gender balance in public appointments and in the governance of public institutions. But once again it is important to be realistic about how much this is likely to achieve when vital policies are outwith the Scottish parliament. One thing that is likely to soon be in Scotland's power is to make sure that women have the best possible access to employment tribunals so cases of sex discrimination can be vigorously contested.

This combination of better advice services, strategies for desegregating employment on gender lines, direct action to create better jobs for women, better childcare and trying to achieve more family-friendly working practices, a gender equality duty in economic development, and better support for challenging sex discrimination is a package of measures which, over time, will change the economic position of women in Scotland. Scotland should aim for a future in which your gender does not indicate what kind of career you are likely to have, how much you are paid, or how well you are treated. Setting out a clear vision of this in itself would make a big difference.

It would be good if it were possible to propose many more means of achieving greater economic equality in Scotland. Where the economic policies which could do this have been exhausted, the use of welfare policies to reinforce this progress could make a big difference. In particular a radical move towards a 'citizens income' would be a major step. A citizens' income is a policy which increases tax take but returns all the increased income to citizens in a flat-rate payment. Eventually this would reach a level where everyone would be assured of a very basic income sufficient to achieve a secure but very basic standard of living. This would replace all benefits and tax credits and would be a giant step forward in greater economic equality. Of course, none of the necessary powers to achieve this are ones Scotland has access to.

Confronting discrimination in Scotland

In the field of economic equality—probably more than any other policy area—it is simply the truth that Scotland's scope for action is severely limited by its lack of powers. However, while economic equality is the first and most important stage in achieving overall equality and while economic inequality is generally the biggest factor underpinning other forms of inequality, it is clearly not the only form or cause of inequality. In recent years there have been great leaps forward in both the cultural and legal acceptance of the experience of groups in society who previously faced endemic discrimination, prejudice, and persecution, and who continue to suffer from patriarchal society. There is now little legal discrimination (that is, part of the law of the country) against people because of race, gender, sexuality, religion and so on. There are definitely what might be described as administrative injustices (such as the inability of gays and lesbians to get equal access to their partner's pension rights or the use of racial profiling in police stop and search), and these can be grievous, hurtful, and alienating. But the days when you can be arrested and jailed because of your beliefs or your sexuality or where you came from are largely gone in Scotland. At the same time, we have seen a substantial improvement in social and cultural attitudes towards these marginalised groups.

This is all to be welcomed. But it does not mean we can be complacent. Many groups such as asylum seekers, disabled people, the lesbian, gay, bisexual, transsexual and intersexual community (LGBTI) continue to face prejudice, discrimination, and violence. And of course many women (who are in no way a minority) also face discrimination and a depressingly large number of women also face sexual violence and domestic abuse which, as well as causing physical harm, undermines women's liberty. This is a question of justice for all of society and all of society must respond. There can be no equality in the face of violence.

All hopes for greater equality must be underpinned by human rights. A rights-based approach to equality creates a strong framework which makes clear to everyone what is acceptable and what is not acceptable in terms of how people are treated legally, administratively, and also culturally. But more than that, a rights-focused approach creates a legal underpinning which gives routes of legal redress when the way that people are treated contravenes acceptable practice. Scotland has enshrined humans rights law in its legal system and this must be supported, strengthened, and used as a legal means of rectifying any instances of continued injustice in public life. Scottish human rights legislation (the Scotland Act and the Human Rights Act) must be protected and proposals for a British Bill of Rights must be opposed.

There should be bolstered support for Scotland's National Action
Plan for Human Rights and it should be linked to the United Nations
Sustainable Development Goals. All of the UK's international human
rights obligations should be written directly into Scotland's domestic
laws. And the participatory democracy discussed in chapter seven should
be used to engage citizens in a deep discussion of how to advance human
rights in Scotland.

But we will not overcome prejudice, discrimination, and violence
through legal means alone. We must also change social attitudes and
practices—the arenas were the unequal distribution and misuse of
power plays out in the everyday. Those in positions of influence should
set a positive example. This too has improved a lot in recent years and
broadcasters, politicians, and senior figures in business and civic society
are much more conscious of what represents inappropriate language on
race, gender, religious affiliation, and sexuality. As a result, the public
are becoming more aware of this issue. Unfortunately, this is not always
true, and at times the language used about for example refugees has been
disappointingly hostile and dehumanising. Society collectively should
continue to exert substantial pressure on those who use this kind of
language. But it should be proportionate—you cannot change attitudes
through criticism alone and if those who wish to see an end to prejudice
and traditional power structures want to change attitudes then they must
bring people with them.

Over the longer term, we should help people's attitudes to change
through our school system. For many decades now there has developed a
very strong understanding and practice in conflict resolution education.
This just means helping people to understand how to resolve conflict
and disagreement through means other than violence, disengagement,
and hatred. Conflict resolution should be something taught to all
school pupils from the earliest possible age. Empathy education is also
developing fast. This simply means teaching pupils how to recognise,
understand, and respect the feelings of others. A good example of the
need to do this is in helping pupils better respond to LGBTI issues and
education on this should be a fundamental part of empathy education
in every school. Finally there is good educational practice on violence
reduction and how to manage feelings such as anger and a lack of self

esteem in ways which do not manifest in hurting others. In tandem with a more equalities and citizenship focussed PSE syllabus, we will begin in the classroom to interrogate and unpick traditional power structures, with analytical tools which will last a lifetime.

These practices—learning to resolve conflict, encouraging empathy, and teaching people alternatives to violent responses—will have benefits for all of society. Violence and aggression have an impact on everyone (young men are most likely to face the direct consequences of violence), but in combination with the other factors of discrimination and constraints faced by groups such as women, ethnic minorities, the disabled, and LGBTI communities, the benefits of reducing aggression and violence would be particularly beneficial. This must, of course, be partnered by the best support systems possible for women, asylum seekers, transgender people and others who are victims of violence.

For a gender-based sexual violence and domestic abuse, support for women's aid shelters and other means of protecting vulnerable women and children need to be properly funded so that professionals can do their job. Evidence shows that women who have suffered from domestic abuse list higher incomes, access to housing, and childcare as priority issues above refuges. But with the introduction of universal credit, with its payments on a household rather than an individual basis, it is likely to make the issue of financial independence for vulnerable women more severe. Below a case is made for a flexible 'social security' fund to be created, of which a part should be dedicated to making sure that victims of domestic abuse can be supported in ways that ensure they are not made to be reliant on their abuser. Another issue which should be tackled is the intimidation and street harassment of women. In chapter 11 it is proposed that community policing should become a joint responsibility of local councils and local police officers. An obligation should be placed on both to develop strategies to reduce street harassment focussing particularly on local circumstances.

For disabled people, the issue of access is still important, with far too many public and private spaces limiting the mobility of disabled people, which has a knock on effect on their confidence and their willingness to participate. Some of the ideas proposed above will include measures to address this directly: a national housing company would have a provision of ensuring that all new homes and the renovation of existing housing stock are disability friendly, with five per cent of homes in Scotland in need of adaptation.

Most young disabled people don't find work after leaving education, and more than half of working age are not in work. This is a massive waste of human potential that should concern us all. The work programme should be changed from a punitive system to one that tries to support those that are finding it most difficult to enter the labour market. For every £1 spent on the DWP's Access to Work £1.60 is received in tax revenue from increased employment. While the responsibility for Access to Work is not currently part of devolution plans, it highlights the societal benefits of increased employment amongst disabled people.

There is debate about whether the issues of economic equality and social equality should be 'lumped together'. Indeed there is debate about whether gender, race, and class inequality should be treated as one broad subject, since any conversation of one should take into account the others as critical factors in privilege. A National Policy Academy could focus debate for all issues of equality, able to organise itself such that different aspects of the wide equality agenda can be treated separately where that is viewed as the best approach, and collectively when possible. Either way, the duty of producing strong gender, economic, and other inequality impact assessments of all public policy should be a key role. Further, a National Policy Academy dedicated to conflict resolution and non-violence (along with international issues and potentially environmental matters) could develop Scotland as an international leader in these issues. Part of its role should be to advise on policy and deliver good practice advice and support to all public agencies and in cases of social conflict.

Protection from poverty

As has been emphasised, Scotland lacks the powers to address fully the many problems of social and economic inequality, but by pursuing measures like those above it can quickly make some progress, and then over the longer term begin to make structural and systemic change.

But this will take time. Until real progress is made and during a time of imposed austerity, the failures of inequality will hit many people in vulnerable positions. Poverty will be a significant problem in Scotland for many years. So Scotland must act.

The overarching means to deal with poverty—and the problems of anxiety and fear faced by those whose economic insecurity leaves them constantly close to poverty—is to create a system which ensures a basic quality of life for all. This is called social security: the knowledge that you can feel secure and protected from destitution by being part of a society. The first way to do this is to create an economy, a housing system, and a strong set of universal public services which build the foundations of a good life for all. In the longer term, creating a Citizens' Income would mean every member of society knows they are secure and can live a decent life. Until then, we are left with a welfare system over which Scotland has next to no control.

The British welfare system is being converted from a safety net to a form of coercion, used to push people into low-paid work or face genuine destitution. It is the opposite of social security—a system of systematic insecurity. It would be very desirable indeed if Scotland could redesign the entire welfare system (and had the full range of tax powers to pay for it). But it doesn't. At best it looks like it will have only the powers to 'top up' existing benefits but have no control whatsoever over the policy.

Very great care must be taken here. The instinct to use these top-up powers will be strong. However, there are very good reasons for caution. The first of these is the cost. Even making pretty minor top-ups to existing payments quickly mounts up to many hundreds of millions of pounds. This comes at a time when the Scottish budget faces severe cuts, which will inevitably lead to cuts in public services. And as these public services are relied on most by the most vulnerable groups, redirecting money away from these services towards benefit top-ups risk doing little more than hitting these groups in different ways.

Of course Scotland can—and should—use tax powers to try to mitigate the worst of the cuts and the worst impacts of austerity. But as was explored in chapter six, Scotland has limited tax powers and can have an influence over only a minority of the tax base. Nor does Scotland have the enormous corporate wealth of London nor its billionaires. Scotland has to raise tax based on its population and the ability of that population to pay more tax. The proposals outlined in chapter six would raise something approaching £750 million, and it was proposed that £500 million of that be used to lessen the impact of cuts. What remains would be insufficient to top up all benefits to a level which would create real social security.

There are also good policy reasons why using benefit top-ups should cause some concern. The inability to influence policy in any way is prime among them. For example, adding say £10 a week to a benefit will do nothing to help an individual if the UK policy control enables it to have that individual's entire benefits withdrawn through sanctions. This is a demand-led policy—the more people face poverty, the more benefits are paid. But Scotland has a fixed budget and does not control the primary policy levers which would cause the increase in demand (for example, through more unemployment or because of in-work poverty). Once a top-up practice is in place it would be virtually impossible for Scotland to alter that practice in the future as Westminster would have forced Scotland to take responsibility for an entire area of social policy which is not Scotland's responsibility and over which Scotland has no control. If Westminster wishes Scotland to take control over welfare, it must devolve all the relevant powers (including the tax base) to Scotland. If it does not wish to devolve welfare then it alone must be held accountable for its decisions.

However, although Scotland should take great care about using benefit top-ups, it cannot shirk responsibility for the wellbeing of its citizens. The failure of the benefits regime does not lie on Scotland's shoulders, but poverty does. The most direct way to help the acute poverty of those who have faced sanctions or the harshest of the benefit cuts (disproportionately affecting women), is to invest in the many ways that are currently used to support people in the most need. This means everything from hardship funds to social work services. The £250 million identified should be used to create a 'social security' fund and that should be used to target support where it is most needed. Funding should be given to those already dealing with the sharp end of poverty to enable them to improve the financial support they can give in cases where people are facing real hunger, cold, or being made homeless. Women in particular are often trapped by a welfare system that does not enable their independence, a particularly serious threat to women affected by domestic abuse. This fund must emphasise the independence of women where it can.

The group which has been hit hardest by the latest round of benefit cuts is the young unemployed. The withdrawal of a whole range of benefits means that not only do young people in Scotland face fewer job opportunities (and those that are available are increasingly low-paid), but if they can't find work they are being penalised further through lack of financial support. This further robs young people of the feeling that they are involved in their society in meaningful and constructive ways.

In chapter 11 it is suggested that there should be a national volunteering programme to support and encourage communities who wish to improve the quality of their environment through, for example, landscaping, creating allotments, or painting houses. This scheme could incorporate the ability to offer a payment to anyone who is unemployed and under 25 who wishes to volunteer (though ideally there would be no age limit). This would not be a job and it would certainly not be compulsory—this is not 'workfare'. But it could offer (for example) a payment of £50 per week for anyone who volunteered for 15 hours. This would not affect benefit payments and so would be entirely additional. The idea of giving unemployed people an opportunity for involvement in their society as a positive way of addressing the isolation of unemployment has been abused in the past through coercion or exploitation. We must find positive, constructive ways for people to be able to stay involved—and the opportunity to get a small financial stipend which would make a real difference to many.

Beyond this, Scotland can do little more than seek to mitigate the impacts of poverty and austerity, for example by providing high-quality, affordable housing. A mass programme of public rental housing as already outlined would be one way that people would be able to gain access to good quality housing which is efficient to heat for affordable rents. This will help. The ability to upgrade existing housing will improve the quality of life (though not reduce costs since the savings in heating are the means through which the improvements would be made). The second way to mitigate the cost of poverty through collective provision is to reduce utility bills through the provision of municipal energy companies, buying energy collectively, and passing the savings on to customers, as discussed previously. This can play some part in addressing the problems of fuel poverty.

The third way to address this issue is through taking a different approach to food. Here, a rights-driven approach can make a substantial difference. The right to housing is enshrined in Scots law—but not the right to food. However, Scotland as part of the UK is a signatory to the International Covenant on Economic Social and Cultural Rights which includes the right to accessible, affordable, and appropriate food. This covenant could be made part of Scots law, providing benefits also for land reform. Putting the right into law means focusing and co-ordinating efforts both by central and local government and by other agencies to achieve this right progressively over time—and it means being prepared to be challenged legally if these efforts are not being made. The right to food does not just mean 'sufficient calories of any description sufficient to keep someone alive', it is a commitment to people having fair access to decent food that will promote health and wellbeing and not just survival.

Once the right of people not to be hungry is enshrined and understood it will give an impetus to consider further the availability of food in communities which have high levels of poverty. In chapters eight and eleven, a model for a different way consumers can access food is discussed. This would be based around a 'community hub' system where people would be able to buy quickly and cheaply, directly from suppliers. This can cut food costs through cutting out middle men. But clearly Scottish suppliers cannot provide the full range of foods throughout the year. A means of providing high-quality staple foods would be to use collective purchasing. This could be done on a voluntary and local basis, but this is unlikely to provide effective universal coverage. So either at municipal level or through a National Food Company, staple foods could be imported in bulk and sold through a hub network at close to cost.

This would help reduce the cost of foods. But in many cases there are deeper problems to do with habits of food preparation or the lack of equipment in the poorest houses to prepare food properly. Here systems of 'collective cooking' could be arranged. There are models where cafes are created which provide basic prepared foods at low or no cost. The subsidy required for sustaining these is small and by providing a public service which anyone can access, the stigma effect of this kind of provision is low.

There are some other ideas on mitigating poverty which could be considered. For example, if a parallel digital currency is introduced (as explored in chapter six), some of this could be targeted directly at those in poverty. Or the idea of a regular payment scheme for food (discussed in chapter eleven), adapted to offer discounts in those payments for those in poverty.

But there are also longer-term, community-based approaches which can help communities which face high levels of poverty to regenerate themselves. The most important concept in the field of community regeneration is now Asset Based Community Development (sometimes known as ABCD). ABCD takes as its starting point that a community can be supported to address its own challenges by unlocking the assets that already exists within that community. In this way, there is a move away from more traditional approaches to community work by focussing on the gifts and strengths of a community, rather than what needs to be done 'to' it or what has 'gone wrong' with it.

Assets are framed in the broadest sense as everything that is present in a community: people, places, and services. However, at the heart of ABCD is the significance of identifying and unlocking the (often hidden) skills, energy, and passions of individuals within the community, as well as nurturing and building on the social relationships that already exist in communities. Using the strengths, talents, and passion already available, people can then start addressing the things that matter to them and developing their own responses to challenges. ABCD places the community at the centre of the process; it is community-driven change responding to community-identified need, and the role of agencies and professionals is limited to that of offering help only when it is asked for and stepping back so that the community leads.

One of the biggest challenges with the implementation of ABCD has come from the narrow interpretation of assets by agencies, with a focus on physical assets: buildings, parks, services. 'Asset mapping' the physical resources of a community is a useful endeavour but, in and of itself, it is missing the aspect which is both empowering and transformative for communities. To be truly effective, ABCD exposes a need for upskilling among agency staff which supports a shift in mindset from one of problem-solver and initiator to that of enabler and supporter. ABCD has its limitations since although the approach supports communities to take ownership of their own solutions, it lacks any political education element or community organising model, meaning communities aren't necessarily supported to start challenging any of the underlying structural problems. This is why community solutions such as this must be supported by the kind of local and participative democracy discussed in chapter six and with the kind of civic education discussed in chapters six and eleven.

One national level action which could be targeted at helping communities with high levels of poverty would be to carefully consider the siting of any of the centres of employment that would be created by any of the new National Companies (or any of the other means of stimulating higher wage employment considered elsewhere in this book). There is much that can be done by stimulating community-led approaches and it is possible to do more to promote local economies in communities facing poverty. But in the end, the best way to help is to give access to decent jobs. If manufacturing industries can be sited near communities with higher levels of poverty or if they can be planned in such a way that there are good transport links between the communities and the jobs, it creates a genuine opportunity for communities to be regenerated through work.

All this will help to tackle poverty and promote equality. However, once again, the depressing reality must be emphasised that there is a limit to what Scotland can do to reverse the impacts of a poverty-creating agenda forced on Scotland from Westminster. It is equally true that this must be accepted by critics, so long as government does not behave as if this absolves it from responsibility—there is much we can so, and we must start now.

Chapter Eleven
A Good Life

Everything in this book has been about life. It has been about how
to create a public sphere—a commons—in which we can live a good
life. About how to invest to create the conditions for a good life. About
how to provide for that life, and how to ensure its security. But, once
these conditions are set, what makes a good life?

First, we must look to our health—life spent in poor health is not a
good life. So what makes for a healthy population? It is determined by
the context in which people live: everything from the impact of global
environmental change, through to how politics create specific social and
economic conditions, to the social and family networks we are supported
by, to the behaviours people adopt, to the genetics with which they are
born. What matters? Everything.

Fortunately, there is substantial evidence now available from decades
of research about the types of politics, policies, interventions, and
contexts that can support a healthy and equitable society. These include
moves such as living income, adequate social security, redistributive
policies, labour market interventions, participatory democracy, better
housing, stronger community control, less pollution, healthier food,
better conditions at work, and more. Which is to say that the real steps
towards better public health come from precisely the sorts of economic
and social change that would be a common weal Scotland. Health is
therefore a strand that runs through every policy idea in this book and
should be seen as a crucial component of all public policy. Where a
policy harms health it should be rethought. The cost of getting health-
promoting policies wrong is not only ill health but the substantial
knock-on costs to the NHS.

Design for living: housing and the town centre

Then; begin where we live. The means for building a new
generation of public rental housing has been discussed in chapters

seven and eight. It is a system that would mean the only limitation on the number of these houses we build would be availability of land and demand. In chapter six the role of a Land Value Tax in controlling the price of land and keeping it closer to its economic value was explained. This should discourage practices such as 'land banking' (where speculative developers buy up and keep land not to develop it but to limit supply and increase price) and make more land available for housing. But more must be done to make sure this land is used for the kind of housing which improves lives and not the kind which is mainly about trapping people in mortgages.

To achieve this, there should be a more aggressive approach to planning permission. At the moment, planning permission seems often to be viewed as a means of creating 'economic growth'. This is just a way of saying 'to make big developers wealthy' by letting them use public policy to increase the value of their assets. Developers buy land and then greatly increase the value of that land by using decisions on planning which are meant to be there to protect the interests of the commons. But instead of protecting those interests, the result is generally overpriced housing on overpriced land in badly designed developments. At times, there seems to be an uncomfortable closeness between those who grant planning permission and those who benefit. Planning should be used much more aggressively in the public interest to promote more affordable housing, more access to land for self-build, and—crucially—more public rental housing. Zoning larger volumes of land exclusively for these purposes and attaching much more stringent criteria on commercial developments will thusly improve access to land.

The housing that is built must be designed for life and designed to last. In chapter eight it was proposed that German-style 'house factories' should be built and that the new generation of houses should be manufactured there. Modern technology means that extremely high performance houses can be built for very modest costs. In fact, passive houses (houses which are so efficient they either don't need to be heated at all or actually generate more energy than they use) can now be produced inexpensively. The regulations for all housing in Scotland should be tightened—our housing is simply unacceptably far behind the standard of performance of modern European housing.

And it's too small. Just as important as the quality of the design and build of the house is the quality of the overall development. The commercial housing sector is designed to maximise profit, and since 'detached villas' are most marketable, the maximum number of houses that meet this description are crammed into the smallest possible area. This is one of the reasons that Britain has one of Europe's smallest average house sizes. In fact, people are every bit as happy living in well-designed higher density housing—some of Scotland's more desirable housing is in large tenements or in spacious terraces. And some of the world's most desirable housing is in tower blocks. People are social and the idea that in all circumstances we want to live in boxes separated from each other is incorrect. Well-designed terraced, tenement, and high-rise developments (as well as some other forms of high-density housing) mean that the living space in houses can be much bigger. People have always liked living in these ways and better communities are formed from well-designed housing.

Properly designed developments also mean there is room for life: parks, open spaces, shops, and cafes. Most modern developments lack all of these things; they have pavements but nowhere to go on them. This means that social interaction is discouraged (shopping, getting to work, going to school—all these things are done in cars). The irony is that all of these 'detached villas' leave you with less space but more isolation. Planning and design should be driven not by how much profit can be made but by the quality of life that can be lived in a house, the strength of community that can be achieved in a development, the beauty of what is built and the positive impact it will have on society and the environment. The 'market' will not do this on its own since positive social impact, strong community, and beauty don't generate profit. There must be much more substantial regulation and intervention in how housing is designed and developed.

But this should certainly not mean tick-box planning. The great cities in the world and the really attractive places to live were the result of design. In both architecture and planning there is excellent knowledge about how design makes developments both beautiful and practical. Our skylines, our communities, our high streets, our city centres—these places are not 'free markets' but part of the commons.

We should exert much more collective and mutual influence over how these developments take place so they don't become sprawl or chaotic or repetitive or unbalanced—or plain ugly. And the proper infrastructure of community life—halls, parks, cafes, shops, schools, nurseries, places to work—would become a central feature of developments.

If the National Policy Academies are set up as proposed in chapter six, one should be focussed on housing and community. That Academy should advise on national and local approaches and strategies which will improve the quality of the design of the places where we live and work. It would also promote new technologies and techniques in housing and house design to ensure that the generation of housing Scotland builds now will stand the test of time.

There are two explicit social (and economic) goals which should be a definitive part of this housing strategy. The first is to control house prices. As discussed previously, house price rises in Britain have been driven not by social need but by financial speculation. Rising house prices is one of the most direct ways that wealth has been transferred from the majority of the population to a minority, and so is at the heart of inequality. Perpetually-rising house prices are very clearly not sustainable. There must be a manageable way to bring house price inflation back under control. Greater housing supply will do that on its own, but even more so if people are given an option of high-quality rental housing and are not left with their only option being to buy houses from commercial developers. Diversity in the housing market will ease the pressures of what has become a sort of cartel in which a very small number of enterprises control most of the housing supply for purely commercial aims. Rent controls in the private rental sector will also have an impact.

The second is the desegregation of housing. The uniform nature of housing developments leads to a uniform pricing of the houses in those developments. This in turn leads to people of a specific income spectrum inhabiting these uniform developments. So we end up with housing estates of high earners, housing estates of high-middle earners, housing estates of low-middle earners and so on. This creates a society which is segregated on the basis of income. We are no longer building mixed communities where we meet people who are not exactly like us. This damages our society and hinders empathy—our ability to understand how other people live and the different sets of issues that affect their lives. If we can build public rental housing which is both so good in quality and so reasonable in price that it is accessible both by people with low incomes and desirable by, for example, young professionals, designed to be attractive to both young and old, we can create mixed communities. From this intermixing, community empathy and cohesion can grow.

One of the problems of encouraging more people to consider renting is the perception of inflexibility and authoritarianism which characterised the management of the 'council house' in the 1960s and 1970s. The new generation of public rental housing should be self-managed by residents at a very local level (the block, the street). Renters should have life-long security of tenure if they want it, and they should have the right to adapt and upgrade their house in much the same way they would if they owned it. Residents associations should manage the upkeep of the fabric of the housing collectively and democratically. Where possible, new developments should include a concierge system so there is a permanent office in each street or block where residents can go for help and support.

In all of this, the pleasantness of where we live has a substantial impact on our psychological wellbeing. If we are surrounded by monotonous drab greys with little sign of greenery, no sense of variation and harmony, it affects us. We feel more drab ourselves. Too much of Scotland appears to have been built with little sense of what it would be like to live there, with street after street of rough grey rendering, and any sign of grass cut to within an inch of its life. Very often these are good, well-built houses (council housing is larger and of a better standard than much of the commercial housing sector) in strong communities. But they are seldom anyone's idea of an attractive environment.

Transforming these environments is not difficult. The houses can be painted – vibrant colours like Tobermory on Mull, or muted shades of sage and lavender. They could be re-rendered in modern finishes, or re-clad in wood. Modern paints and technologies have extremely long lives. Public land around houses can be landscaped with trees and flowers. Paths and fences can be revived and replaced. The places we live can be bright, attractive, enjoyable places to live. We do not need to tolerate grim.

A National Housing Policy Academy could develop a national plan for 'de-grimming' and revitalising the infrastructure of communities. People can be encouraged to think about what they'd like their community to look like. The new layer of genuinely local councils should be given the responsibility of asking every community, housing estate, and street, how they'd like to improve and revitalise their community. They would have to help in providing the labour, and the council would have to help in providing materials. The young unemployed can be given payments to encourage them to get involved (mentioned briefly in chapter ten). People can be trained to carry out much of the work themselves. This is not about removing the responsibility of existing authorities to maintain the social fabric, but about improving things beyond that basic responsibility. We think of Scotland as a beautiful country, but when we think of it we think of hills and glens and beaches, and sometimes of historic towns and parts of cities. Why do we accept that, when we think of Scotland as being beautiful, we seldom think of where we live? Why don't we change that?

Another aspect of our towns that we need to think about is the role of the town centre. Thought has already been given to what might be done in the immediate term to address the changing nature of how we use our town centres now that more and more shopping is done online or in out-of-town developments. It seems very likely that this trend will continue and that there will be substantial changes in what a town centre is for and how it is used. Preventing decline is of course important but we need to think beyond that. Will there ever be as many small retailers again? Can we sustain more economic activity if we follow a plan of localising consumption and production? If shop units are no longer viable as shops, might they become service hubs? Or be repurposed for micro and craft manufacture? Could they become shared facilities such as workshops or studios where people could get free or inexpensive access to tools? Might new working practices mean they can be hot-desks from which remote and home workers can work? Should they become where we run our childcare? Might they become spaces that help and support activism and hobbies? Do they become the place where a 'ting' meets?

Social and economic trends appear to be moving in opposite directions. What used to draw us into the city (large scale industries) is largely gone, and there is every scope for disaggregating the economy out across towns and even villages. At the same time, online retail and banking means that many of the services we expected to have in our town are not needed to the same extent. We are seeing an end to the need for spacial concentrations (lots of people in one place) at the same time as an increase in the concentration of services away from 'spaces' altogether. There is a case for taking a 'nextgen' strategy and having a large and participative national review of what town centres, towns, villages and cities should be like in decades to come—and how best we can get there.

Another area directly linked to how towns and cities work is transport. As has been mentioned, transport infrastructure in Scotland is not particularly good and is seen by most as being substantially behind the European average. The problem is that it takes a substantial amount of time to put transport infrastructure in place and it is likely that by the time Scotland caught up with European norms, transport technology would have moved on again and Scotland would still be well behind the world leaders. There is therefore a strong case for Scotland taking a 'nextgen' strategy here as well. This would look at what the next generation of technologies would enable, look at how they would work in a Scottish context, and plan now for implementing them as part of a redesign of Scottish transport.

Deconsumerisation

By looking at housing, communities, town centres, and transport in this way, we create a foundation for people to live a good life. But what we do with our lives is equally important. Me-first economics has created a cycle of work-to-consume. Saturation advertising and marketing continuously pushes us to spend money. But since me-first economics has also created long-term stagnation in wages, it has required us to borrow more and more to fuel consumption (personal debt in Britain is back to record levels). We are then trapped by our debt into maximising income in a low-pay economy, which often means excessive working hours (we work among the longest hours in Europe and have among the fewest holidays). And then we are actively told that if this makes us feel a bit down, we should lift our spirits and cheer ourselves up by consuming more.

The harmful effects of this cycle are well-documented. It creates stress and anxiety, generates low self-esteem, harms our physical health, damages our social relations (particularly inside the family), and harms the environment. But it has made a lot of powerful people very rich indeed and they have created a system where politicians and the media now routinely accept constantly increasing consumption as not only a sign of success but an essential driver of the economy. We need a different approach. Of course consumption is an essential component of the economy but we need to think much more clearly about what we consume, and how.

Scotland should set out a national strategy for deconsumerisation. The overarching aim should be to reduce the extent to which the value of its citizens is measured by their ability to repeatedly purchase short-life, disposable consumer goods and rely on the symbolism provided by these good to define their status in society; who they are and where they belong. Addressing these issues will reduce the destructive burden of consumerism on the environment, reduce the emotional burden of never ending insecurity on consumers, and reduce the debt burden required to purchase goods with little or no longevity or material worth.

Hobbies, sport, the arts, social life, entertainment, learning—all of these things make us feel better. They also all have positive economic impacts. But because they are much less effective at parting us with our money and transferring it to multinational corporations, they are seldom promoted and in some cases discouraged. It is in our common interest that we make that transition and so we need the commons to rebalance the power of advertising which pushes us in the other direction.

We must make activism and participation possible. A good transport system, proper systems of local democracy, reducing working hours, and creating supportive infrastructure such as childcare will make it easier for us to do things and get involved. Then we must make participation cheaper. All the facilities which are in the public realm (swimming pools, gyms, sports halls, outdoor activities in parks, museums) should be priced not on the basis of what the commercial sector is able to charge for the same activities, but on the basis of what will increase their use and open them up to everyone. They should not be seen as an income-generating device for cash-strapped local authorities. It would be much better to pay a little more in local tax and then let people do things inexpensively.

There are other ways in which the cost of participation can be reduced. Activities such as DIY need tools, but few people do enough DIY to really justify buying these tools (the average lifetime usage of a screwgun is less than 15 minutes, the rest of its lifetime, it gathers dust). We can create 'share shops' or tool libraries in which people can borrow tools or other creative goods for short periods, inexpensively or for nothing. These goods would be of higher quality and would be repairable, challenging the throwaway culture. From borrowing fruit presses for people who want to make their own cider to being able to access good sewing machines for people interested in dressmaking to borrowing mountaineering equipment to hiring a bike or borrowing a board game—the illogical and often prohibitive capital cost of being active can be removed.

Many of the things that people enjoy doing require space. For example, there are very big waiting lists for community allotments and many more people would love to be able to grow their own fruit and veg or flowers. Councils should make more land available for these purposes—and once a land strategy brings the cost of land down, more land should be purchased and dedicated to these purposes.

We have also lost many communal spaces such as football pitches, community halls or local sports centres, often in favour of one large, centralised, and expensive facility. This is bad planning and should be reversed. Some Community Sports Hubs, like at the Common Wealth Games site, seem to be more interested in getting people in from the wealthy suburbs around Glasgow to pay to play badminton and football than those who live in the East End. If we want people to take part in regular physical exercise through sport we have to make it affordable, and therefore local sporting facilities should be made as cheap as possible or even free for those living in the local area. We need to break down gender segregation in sporting activity as well. Women's football is the fastest growing sport nationally and across the world, yet funding for this is paltry compared to that of the men's game. Sporting activity doesn't just improve physical health, the social activity involved in sport has been proven to make people happier and reduce mental illness.

Learning is popular. Many people would like to learn a language or dressmaking or car maintenance or an introduction to Scottish history. Learning has steadily been transformed into something provided only as a means of training people for work. This should also be reversed. Formal training providers such as colleges should be encouraged to provide much more open-access learning opportunities. The constant development of e-learning means Scotland could develop a national library of online learning. A national skills database could help match people who want to learn with people who already have the skills. And there is much scope for peer learning where groups of people get together and learn together.

Participation in the arts is also a big part of learning. Whether it is learning to play guitar, singing in a choir, painting, or writing, formal and informal learning opportunities can help people be active. We can create lots of open access and shared facilities. Every town could have free rehearsal space for what people need to rehearse as a band or perhaps to write and record their own music. Empty shops could be converted into art studios or editing suites where people could borrow cameras and then film and edit their own films.

Public policy should then see marketing as a facilitator, not a manipulator. The legal regulation of advertising and marketing is not within Scotland's powers, but all public agencies have control over public space and many aspects of sponsorship. Ideally all advertising targeted at children should be banned. Certainly everything possible should be done to remove or minimise advertising in and around schools (including commercial sponsorship or provision of educational materials). The public sector should not be encouraging advertising and should not be planning it into new developments. The same spaces can be used for social or cultural purposes. Other forms of consumption which have particularly negative health and environmental impacts should also be challenged, for example, where possible the cost of removing litter should be passed on to the enterprise causing the litter.

All of this does not mean that deconsumerisation is simply a drain on the economy. There are alternative ways people can spend money in the economy which are better for the economy and better for them. For example, domestic tourism is a very effective way to recycle wealth throughout the Scottish economy. A domestic tourism strategy which encouraged people not to buy pointless consumer goods but instead to travel and stay across the country and be active would have very substantial economic and health benefits.

Food sovereignty

One thing we will always have to consume is food. But whether this kind of consumption is life-enhancing or life-harming is up to us. In chapter eight the positive economic impact of a more localised food system was explored and chapter nine looked at how food 'sovereignty' could be achieved. But the same system can improve the way we eat and the quality of the food we eat. If we are providing more food through local production and distribution, then we are reducing the share of the market taken up by the harmful, low-quality, and highly processed foods which are heavily marketed to us—the promotion and sale of which should be restricted in all public facilities and especially schools.

A way to encourage a shift from bad food to good food is to help people resist the constant marketing of food based on instant gratification. The marketing of food is particularly reliant on impulse purchasing with big displays of beautifully photographed, tempting products explicitly designed to try and get us to buy not only more than we intended to buy, but specifically to buy high-fat and high-sugar products we had no intention of buying before we reached the supermarket. Other marketing techniques such as bulk deals and selective product discounting are designed to give us the impression that we're achieving value for money. But we're not—because one third of the food we buy is wasted precisely because of impulse purchasing of food we don't need. Supermarkets want us to be capricious shoppers, because capricious shoppers waste a lot of money.

We can encourage different approaches. We don't buy electricity as we go along; we commit to ensuring stability of supply and spread payments evenly. We could do something similar for food. Shoppers could be given the option of a 'good food card' which would be supported by lots of local producers and suppliers. Direct debits would load these cards up with money each month and then they could be used to buy food from 'hub' shops and local suppliers. Ensuring this consistency of market would enable local producers and suppliers to plan ahead and establish stable, reliable businesses (capricious shopping is great for processed foods laden with preservatives, not for sustaining virtuous local food markets). The result would be a greatly increased availability of good quality food— small craft bakers at the end of your street would be possible again. Such a move could transform our relationship to food, improving not only the economy and our health but the quality of our lives too.

But good food is not just about how much sugar or fat is in it, but also to do with how it was produced (animal welfare, labour conditions, climate change impact, soil and water stewardship, biodiversity—in a word agroecological) and how it is traded (fair margins, transparency etc.). Short food chains are a key part of that. We need to keep coming back to the truth that feeding everyone well in Scotland is easy given how much food we produce, and we could produce the same amount more sustainably. The key is rethinking the food system as a public concern like education, housing, and health—not simply a market to be regulated in the lightest possible way.

Supporting a creative Scotland

Art and culture enrich our lives. They make us happy (and sad and excited and angry). They make us laugh (and cry and scream and fall in love). It might be your favourite musical or a comedy gig, a play or a rock concert, an open mic night at your local pub or an art gallery. But it might also be a poem you read on a bus or a photograph you see in a window. Too often art and culture are presented as if they are just for the 'elite'—as if the music you listen to, the films you watch, and the pictures on your walls aren't art. But once again, me-first economics is only interested in art which can make large profits and sees art only as a consumer good. That is why commons must support the production of art.

But before we can have art, we need artists. One of the most effective ways we could create an upsurge of Scottish art would be if we could introduce a Citizens' Income scheme. That would allow artists (many of whom have to survive on very low incomes from their work, particularly in the early years of their career) to live tolerable lives while they develop. Until that is possible, we should not only dedicate more funding towards the arts in general, we should shift the balance away from supporting works of art and towards supporting artists. Project funding is essential for large scale productions such as opera or stage plays, or for large exhibitions, and Scotland should be ambitious in always trying to expand the number of these we invest in every year. But for many artists, what they really need is time and support to be able to produce art. Project grant funding may not be the way to do this, and is definitely not suitable for the variety of creative mediums artists work in. If we want more artists, we need to make it possible for more people to survive being an artist. A scheme where artists could apply for a modest but secure monthly income which enabled them to focus on their art could make an enormous difference.

Once we have more art, we should aim to get more people actively engaged as audiences. This should begin at school. The importance of making people 'comfortable' with the environment in which art takes place is enormous. The etiquette of an art gallery ('is it okay to look at the pictures really close up?') or a concert hall ('when am I supposed to clap?') or the architecture of a theatre ('what's a dress circle?') is not complicated—but it can feel complicated and alienating if you've never been. Every school child should get a chance to attend a wide range of arts performances and exhibitions, not just to let them find out what they enjoy, but also so they can become confident when they decide to come back on their own.

There are other ways we can get more people into audiences, one of which is greater utilisation of what is already there. The marginal cost of adding a few more performances is not high. These could then be marketed directly to people who don't usually go—at a substantially reduced cost. Another is to get transport systems right so it is easy for people outside of cities to get to performances, perhaps offering special bus services for communities. And more public support in encouraging people to attend through knowing what's on would be invaluable, perhaps with an online listing service covering the whole of Scotland.

One substantial intervention that cannot go ignored is reviving plans for a Scottish digital broadcast channel. Film and TV provides work for many artistic practices obviously including actors and the wide range of film and broadcast trades, but also for writers, artists, set designers, composers, musicians, costume designers, and more. Once a Scottish channel was in place, one major strand of its work should be to commission films for Scottish audiences. Filmmaking in Scotland simply lacks any serious critical mass and very few career options. Until we make more films we simply won't develop the infrastructure, skills, and experience which will enable us to produce a reliable flow of commercially successful films for a global audience (in the way Scandinavian film and TV has).

Attending sport also improves people's lives, but it can be expensive. Professional football is another area where community control—control by the fans—is much more likely to produce sustainable, well-run clubs that are affordable for fans and play a positive role in the local area. There has been numerous examples of clubs exploiting fan loyalty (they aren't, generally, going to join the competitors), which is a form of monopoly control. Fans should have a right to take clubs into fan ownership if a majority vote in favour of it. Albion Rovers of Coatbridge have innovated in this respect, offering a pay-what-you-can scheme in 2014 for the first time, which seen record season ticket sales and record attendance at games, leading the team on to win in their league, with money left over to renovate their modest stadium.

In general, activism, arts, sport, and participation should be taken more seriously in public policy. Me-first politics sees these 'leisure time' activities as being the business of the consumer and the market and believes that public policy should largely stay out of it. Of course, me-first politics doesn't really want to distract us from shopping. There is a strong case for one of the National Policy Academies to be dedicated to developing ideas, policy and practice in these areas and to support the development of all the arts.

Justice and policing for quality of life

Some will argue that all of this focus on enhancing quality of life will mean little to people whose life is blighted by immediate social problems. While there are arguments in favour of the vital emotional and social benefits of such accessible pastimes, we must also take into account that further action must be taken to ensure access. Approaches to poverty and community development and also to prejudice and discrimination were explored in chapter ten. However, some communities have higher levels of crime than others and this crime (or often the fear of this crime) really can blight people's lives. It is hard to achieve a good quality of life if you're afraid of your own neighbourhood or every time you try to improve it, it is vandalised.

There is a strong case for arguing that criminal justice is a quality of life issue. It is about protecting individuals from violence or the loss of or damage to property, making them feel safe and secure where they live, and protecting their environment from vandalism. However, most people tend to see criminal justice as a process of punishment and recompense for harm done. Of course, the very concept of justice does inherently imply that we should face consequences for our actions—and we should. But if the focus of criminal justice is seen as improving the quality of people's lives through greater security, it changes the emphasis.

A focus on quality of life necessitates a long term view: punishing someone for harming people's lives will mean little if they return and cause that harm again and again. So in the end, long-term cannot be achieved by trying to exclude anyone who does 'bad things' (which might mean violent crime, but it might also mean failing to pay a bill or stealing food in desperation) from society. This seems to be the approach taken in the American justice system, where repeat offending is met with long or indeed lifelong jail sentences. This system cannot be said to have worked in almost any way (there are only a very few exceptions with people who, taking into account mental health and psychological issues, seem to be beyond rehabilitation, and who are genuine dangers to society).

For everyone else, we should use whatever approach is shown best to reduce criminality. And the evidence suggests that this is seldom jail. Of course, for many the best preventative method is to make sure they themselves have decent lives—decent income in cohesive communities where they can live with self-respect. That is the primary aim of all-of-us-first politics. But where that hasn't happened or where it has failed, there should as far as possible be a presumption against jail. Certainly there should be an end to short jail sentences which do more harm than good by putting people who may have committed fairly minor crimes into an environment which exposes them to a culture of worse criminality. There are a whole host of ways to ensure reasonable recompense for wrongs done, which encourage some payback to communities they may have harmed and which—crucially—help to rehabilitate offenders and give them the best possible chance of avoiding reoffending. And a national focus on violence reduction and conflict resolution as discussed in chapter ten would make a major difference.

Along with rehabilitation practices, it would be worth looking at the Scottish court system to explore whether it is working as well as it should be. Justice and the law remains a comparatively closed practice and it is not necessarily the case that all aspects of the court system primarily work towards social benefit. Criminal justice is always a thorny subject in which public opinion can be fairly reactionary. An open and broad-based National Justice Policy Academy could undertake a large scale participatory process partly to develop better approaches to criminal justice but also to engage the public in thinking about what is really in their long term interests. Emphasising punishment is probably not it.

The other half of crime prevention is policing. There has been much controversy about the structure and operation of policing in Scotland. Resolving this will be easier if there is a focus on at what level the most effective policing takes place. The number of serious crimes or crimes with a national or large geographical area which benefit from centralised policing are small—probably less than ten per cent of police business. For these, a single national force may make sense. But for the other 90 per cent, national policing obviously isn't appropriate, and it is not necessarily the case that regional-level policing makes all that much more sense. For a very large proportion of police work, the relevant scale is the community.

Rather than reorganising policing by breaking up a single national force, a more effective approach would be to allow national policing to continue to cover serious crime but to devolve policy and management of community policing to communities. Local policing should be empowered to work with the new lowest layer of local councils to develop policing strategies which are tailored to local needs. Local police and local councils can then design their approaches without the need for centralised intervention. Crime prevention, community safety, and community cohesion would be the primary goals—moving away from forms of policing associated with criminalisation, like stop-and-search, would be the ultimate aim.

Educating for the common weal

In the end, while quality of life will be heavily influenced by many external factors, it will eventually come down to our own abilities to be happy people. In this we must look at how we learned when we were young, and how we learned to be who we are. Chapter six explored education as a part of the commons. Chapter seven touched on the role of citizenship education in democracy. Chapter eight examined some of the economic roles of education. And chapter ten suggested that education can reduce inequality, prejudice and violence. But education should, at heart, be about improving our quality of life.

This can mean many things. It can mean exposing us to ideas and thoughts which expand how we see ourselves and our lives. It can mean learning coping skills to help us respond positively to the things that happen to us throughout our lives. It can mean giving us the skills to do the things we enjoy. It certainly means making us feel good about ourselves as valuable members of society. It certainly shouldn't mean creating a system driven by the need to pass exams as the means of avoiding a bad life. The cycle of pressure and anxiety that an educational regime driven by testing exerts has been shown to change the brain chemistry of children and can effect them throughout their lives. You cannot test a child into being a happy, constructive, and productive citizen.

Education should be an empowering time when children don't just learn but learn how to learn for themselves. Of course there are certain learn but learn how to learn for themselves. Of course there are certain core skills (literacy and numeracy), and of course education should prepare for work—both those who will go straight from school into work, and those who prepare for further learning. But there are virtually no areas of work remaining which rely on a child's ability to memorise answers and no further learning which expects it. So it is a pointless cruelty to create a system which drives a child's development in these directions.

If there are to be formal tests applied in schools they should be held until the very end of school—or better still, should become entrance exams in the trades or learning institutions they go on to after school. Assessment is necessary to be able to support development, but it should be continuous assessment based on a holistic approach to development.

Otherwise, we should be creating a school system not structured along the fairly arbitrary lines of this subject or that subject. Pupils should learn in mixed groups through project work which cuts across many subjects. In this process, pupils should learn how to draw learning out of their experience. The attributes we should hope for are curiosity, creativity, empathy, and understanding. Being exposed to big ideas, to the sweep of history, to art and literature, to how technologies or plants or our bodies work, how food is grown and cooked, how our society functions—these forms of knowledge will produce children who can be happy and interested in their own lives and the world around them. From there, they can do anything they want.

If politics isn't about the quality of our lives, what is it about? And if it reduces the quality of our lives to how much we possess and consume, how can politics possibly imagine we can be happy, well-rounded people? A common weal Scotland would see collective wellbeing and quality of life as the origin and endpoint of all policy—we should be fearless in working together to achieve it.

CHEERIO

...for now. Because whether you thought the ideas in this book light up a path to the Scotland you want to live in, or whether you believe our path should lie elsewhere, we won't get there by always doing what we always did. If the Scotland imagined in these pages is where you want to live, come and help Common Weal discuss the details further and then campaign for it. If you have different ideas, let's talk. Above all what we hope is that these ideas show that Scotland's future does not need to be the same as Scotland's present. 'Too difficult' or 'that's not how we do things' are poor reasons for doing nothing. Demand better from your politics and your society. Demand ideas—because ideas shape the future. And Scotland and its people really do deserve a better future.